WHAT DOES THE BIBLE SAY ABOUT...?

Question and Answer Time

with

Howard and Lucile Sugden

Edited by Leona Hertel

KREGEL PUBLICATIONS
Grand Rapids, Michigan 49501

What Does the Bible Says About. . .? by Howard F. and
Lucile Sugden, © 1987 by Kregel Publications, a division
of Kregel, Inc. All rights reserved.

Library of Congress Cataloging-in-Publication Data

Sugden, Howard F.
    What Does the Bible Say About. . .?

    Includes indexes.
        1. Theology—Miscellanea. 2. Bible—Examinations,
    questions, etc. I. Sugden, Lucile. II. Title.

BR96.S93 1987   230'.61   87-33869

ISBN 0-8254-3759-8

1 2 3 4 5 Printing/Year 92 91 90 89 88 87

Printed in the United States of America

CONTENTS

PUBLISHER'S PREFACE

The original tapes of these Question and Answer Sessions were edited by Leona Hertel, who for 25 years was personal secretary to Dr. M. R. De Haan, founder and teacher of Radio Bible Class. She has preserved the warm and intimate spirit of the Sugdens as reflected in their informal method of Bible teaching by the use of questions and answers.

Their accumulated Bible knowledge and teamwork in teaching continues to bless and encourage all to whom they minister. Their special way of mixing a little of the "light side" with more serious matters makes learning a delightful experience.

Our prayer is that the contents of this volume will help you discover that there are biblical answers to questions which may have long perplexed you, and you didn't know whom to ask.

TO OUR READERS

The content of this book was made possible through the use of a question box at Muskoka Baptist Conference, Huntsville, Ontario (Canada). The questions came over a period of years, and we are grateful to the hundreds of folk who made use of the "the little red box."

The nature of the meetings was such that we did not have commentaries, reference volumes, or word studies available. We are confident, however, that the Word of God is God's answer to all our questions. Therefore, we "commend you to God, and to the word of his grace, which is able to build you up, and to give you an inheritance among all them which are sanctified" (Acts 20:32).

Pastor and Mrs. Sugden

FOREWORD

During the 1970's and 1980's, Dr. and Mrs. Howard F. Sugden have encouraged people of all ages to write out their questions and deposit them in a "Little Red Box." A feature of their annual three weeks of summer ministry at Muskoka Baptist Conference in Ontario, Canada, has been the daily period of Bible answers to all manner of enquiries. The sessions have been recorded, transcribed by ten volunteer secretaries and now published as a rich treasure of practical Bible insight.

The questions asked reflect the confidence of all ages and the high value placed upon the judgment of those answering. You will sense a unique blend of commitment to Christian principles and lifestyle, tempered by genuine compassion and empathy.

The subjects which have concerned the questioners have followed distinct trends from year to year. The issues are current, reflecting earnest searching for the revealed will of God. You will sense the incisive perception of two leaders who have "understanding of the times", who have confidence that biblical morality is essential and satisfying for the needs of all... men, women, and youth...TODAY. The text and indexing will help the younger readers, just as preachers will treasure the sermonic content and clear, biblical homiletical outlining.

This book distils the wisdom, wit and insight of a man and a woman of God. Howard and Lucile Sugden exemplify creative, refreshing independence as well as a rich harmony of purpose and service. They have been growing together through more than 50 years of diligent personal research, biblical preaching and teaching, and pastoral counselling.

Dr. Sugden is a "people person." In his three pastorates and at Bible conferences in many countries, he has "welcomed the saints" by shaking hands for the half-hour leading into every preaching service. He is tuned to the times. Honored by the capital city of the state of Michigan as "Lansing's Citizen of the Year," his clear presentation of truth has caused him to be in demand in pulpits, as a frequent guest lecturer at Michigan State University and scores of other campuses.

May this compendium of applied theology challenge every reader to acknowledge the relevance and authority of the Word of God.

"A good man [and lady] out of the good treasure of the heart bringeth forth good things..." — *Matthew 12:35*

Richard D. Holliday

1
BAPTISM

1. Baptized for the Dead

The words "baptized for the dead" in 1 Corinthians 15:29 are confusing. Can you make this passage clearer?

Dr. Sugden: The verse reads: "Else what shall they do which are baptized for the dead, if the dead rise not at all? Why are they then baptized for the dead?" (1 Cor. 15:29). The only way I can make this verse more clear is to tell you what I personally think it means. The apostle Paul saw death thinning the ranks of the early church, just as it does in our church today. In 30 years of ministry, I have probably buried 400 of my people. I always pray that God will fill the ranks with other godly people.

This is probably what the apostle Paul said. When someone died, there were new people who were being baptized, not in the place of the dead, but to take the place of those that had died.

The Mormon Church has misused this verse. By the way, if you want to study a cult that is absolutely devastating, I think the Mormon group is probably the most dangerous in our land today. The more I study, the more I am concerned about the growth of Mormonism. They baptize for the dead.

In his book on First Corinthians, Harry Ironside said that he talked with someone who told him about a man who had been baptized thousands of times. He had been baptized for all the crownheads of Europe, all the leaders of the world. He was baptized for the dead, which is as utterly and absolutely ridiculous as the whole Mormon philosophy.

2. Immersion

Will you please comment on baptism by immersion compared to infant baptism?

Mrs. Sugden: They ask a Baptist to do that!

Dr. Sugden: Here on the Muskoka Lake Grounds they call our boat *Total Immersion*.

Mrs. Sugden: If you study church history, you will find that the early church did immerse. I had a professor of church history who was a Methodist. He said there is no doubt that the early church immersed, but when the church started to believe that baptism was necessary for salvation, they started sprinkling babies. They first baptized by immersion, but later they sprinkled because they thought it was necessary for a baby to be baptized to be saved. The Greek church still immerses babies.

Dr. Sugden: The word "immerse" means "to put under." I was on a bus one day, and the fellow sitting next to me was reading a Greek newspaper. I asked him, "How are things going?"

He said, "Fine."

Then I said, "You're a Greek, aren't you?"

He answered, "Yes."

I said, "I notice you are reading your paper. It looks interesting. Are you a Greek Catholic?"

"Oh, yes," he said. "I am a Greek Catholic."

I asked him, "What is the difference between your church and the Roman Catholic Church?"

He told me, "One of the differences is that they sprinkle, and in our church we dunk." I thought that was good.

The New Testament is the only real authority for church procedure. It is not what we work out in our meetings or profound gatherings. There is not one instance in the New Testament of an infant ever being baptized.

Baptism is for believers, and so in our church we call it "believer's baptism." That's exactly what it is, and we do exactly as they did in the New Testament. We immerse them in the name of the Father, the Son, and the Holy Spirit.

The other night one of my assistants was doing the baptizing. One of our candidates was a fellow 6′ 7″ tall. The pastor said to me, "Tonight I think I'd be glad to be a Presbyterian."

3. Infant Baptism

Is there any scriptural basis for infant baptism? And how did it start?

Mrs. Sugden: Infant baptism did not start until way after the early church. It began after the belief that baptism was a part of salvation called "baptismal regeneration." During the time of Constantine, the church believed that baptism was so important that they taught it should be a part of salvation. If it is a part of salvation, they felt, then all babies should be baptized. Infant baptism started about the year 359 A.D.

Dr. Sugden: Infant baptism is not biblical. You remember that when Philip and the Ethiopian eunuch met, they came to much water. He said, "What does hinder me to be baptized, because there is much water?" Philip said to him, "If thou believest, thou mayest." In other words, "You have to believe first, before you are baptized."

"And as they went on their way, they came unto a certain water: and the eunuch said, See, here is water; what doth hinder me to be baptized? And Philip said, If thou believest with all thine heart, thou mayest. And he answered and said, I believe that Jesus Christ is the Son of God. And he commanded the chariot to stand still: and they went down both into the water, both Philip and the eunuch; and he baptized him" (Acts 8:36–38).

2
BIBLE INTERPRETATION

4. Aaron and Miriam

In Numbers 12:1 Miriam and Aaron spoke against Moses. Then in verse 10 Miriam became leprous because of this sin. Why wasn't Aaron punished too? This is not a "women's lib" question, but one of fairness.

Dr. Sugden: Was God fair? As you read the whole story of Miriam and Aaron and their relationship, you discover that Miriam was probably dealt with more harshly because she was responsible for the insurrection. She started it. This is indicated because in this context it speaks of her first. Because she was responsible, she bore the punishment.

5. A.D. and B.C.

When we talk about B.C. and A.D., when actually does A.D. start? Was it when Christ was born, or was it after His death? My family Bible lists many of the events and the year they happened: for example, A.D. 7 and 8, Jesus at the age of 12 visited the temple; A.D. 27, Jesus baptized. A 14-year-old girl asked this question. She was taught that time stood still in a sense between Christ's birth (B.C.) until His death (A.C.). I had never given it any thought before, so really couldn't answer her.

Dr. Sugden: Neither did the person who told her this. Normally time measurement began with the birth of Christ. Everything that came before Him was B.C., everything that came since is A.D.

Isn't it staggering that when a Baby was dropped in a manger, He held up His little arms and stopped history. He is the focal point of history. Everything before Him was B.C. and everything since He came is A.D. He is before all things, and by Him all things hold together—time, history, everything!

6. Adam and Eve

In Genesis 3:21 we read that God made clothes for Adam and Eve from the skins of animals. Adam and Eve knew nothing about death and dying. Do you suppose God allowed them to see Him take the life of an animal? If so, they would see another side of God as a judge.

Dr. Sugden: I'm not too sure about the question. I would presume that Adam and Eve—who were normal people mentally, physically, and emotionally—were aware that God had taken the life of an animal in order for them to have clothing.

I would also presume that they may already have had some knowledge that this had to do with the way God was going to cover and repair the sin they had committed. I believe this because of Abel, who offered to God, by faith, a sacrifice. He saw the Cross, and he saw Calvary.

I think that Adam and Eve probably knew something about it too.

7. The Ark

How did God climate-control the ark? Please tell us a good book on the ark suitable for a keen teenager.

Dr. Sugden: First of all, God made the ark in such a way that it was air-conditioned. Did you know that?

It was a three-story building, 450 feet long and 75 feet wide. It was six times as long as it was wide. Noah finished off each floor within a foot-and-a-half of the top. There were no boards around that foot-and-a-half, so just think of all the air space they had on each floor.

The ark didn't have windows, but each floor was air-conditioned. Every morning, when Noah pushed the button and those things came rolling down and gave them all that air, it was absolutely perfect.

The best book on the Ark is the Bible. You knew that, didn't you? You have to be smart to know things like this, because you have to construct with your own imagination, all the wonders of the ark. I'm a lover of books, but I do not know of any book that is specifically written on the subject of the Ark.

If you have a good imagination, however, you can delight children with the account of the ark and how it was built. For example, I have Noah on the phone, calling the lumber yard to order the material. He tells them to send up 450 two by fours. The man on the other end of the phone says, "I've got a nut on the phone. He wants 450 two by fours. He's building an ark. What's an ark?"

You have all the wonders of it. Let your imagination be confined to the Bible, but just let it roam.

Pastor Warren Wiersbe tells me, "Howard, don't forget the wonder of imagination in preaching."

It's a great thing to have imagination in preaching, circumscribed by the Word of God. There's so much room to do it. That's why God didn't put it in piece by piece by piece. He didn't tell Noah to get so many two by fours. He wants us to have imagination, confined within the Word of God.

8. The Book of Life

Revelation 3:5 says, "He that overcometh, the same shall be clothed in white raiment; and I will not blot out his name out of the book of life, but I will confess his name before my Father, and before his angels." Are there people whose names could be blotted out?

Mrs. Sugden: There are two books: the Book of Life, and the Lamb's Book of Life. I believe that everyone who is born is in the Book of Life. If you reject Christ, your name is blotted out. The one who overcomes is the one who believes. This is what John is saying here. So a believer will not be blotted out. He will still be in the Book of Life, and he will also be in the Lamb's Book of Life.

Dr. Sugden: Yes, he will have his name in two books: the Book of Life, and the Lamb's Book of Life.

By the way, someone came to me and said, "Pastor, we've touched so many areas in these Question and Answer times. I have more new thoughts than I've ever had in my life."

Well, that's what we're supposed to do—create an inquiry into the Word of God. You say, "I can't wait to get my Bible dictionary and my Bible and start working."

Do a little study sometime on the Book of Life and the Lamb's Book of Life. In Psalm 139, the psalmist said: "I will praise thee; for I am fearfully and wonderfully made: marvelous are thy works; and that my soul knoweth right well. My substance was not hid from thee, when I was made in secret, and curiously wrought in the lowest parts of the earth" (Psalm 139:14,15).

He said, "Before I was born." This is pre-natal. "Thine eyes did see my substance, yet being unperfect; and in thy book all my members were written. . ." (Psalm 139:16a).

That's an amazing thing! I came across this as I was reading this psalm and thinking about God, His omnipotence, His omniscience, and His omnipresence. Suddenly David dropped this in. He said that before I was ever born and was imperfect ". . . in thy book all my members were written, which in continuance were fashioned, when as yet there was none of them" (Psalm 139:16b).

In other words, before I was born, God put my name in the Book. So, according to this passage, I believe that our names are placed in the Book even before we are born.

Then when God deals with us by His Spirit, if we refuse Him, our names are removed from the Book.

Mrs. Sugden: That gives us proof that babies are saved.

Dr. Sugden: We believe that babies and those who die before the age of accountability go to heaven because of the adequacy of the work of Jesus Christ on Calvary.

It is possible to have our name blotted out of the Book of Life, but never out of the Lamb's Book of Life. The Lamb's Book of Life is the book in which our names are inscribed when we come to know the Lord Jesus as Savior. We are in that Book forever.

9. The City Gate

Please comment on what the "city gate" is in Proverbs 31:23, 31 as it relates to the wife of noble character. What would be the parallel for this place in our day? "Her husband is known in the gates. . ." (Prov. 31:23). ". . . let her own works praise her in the gates" (Prov. 31:31).

Dr. Sugden: In the States we have counties. Mrs. Sugden and I live in Ingham County, and the town of Mason is our county seat. That is the center of government for our county. Lansing is the center of government for our state, as you have Ottawa in Ontario.

In the Old Testament, the gate of the city was the place where all the business transactions were made. This is where the officials met, discussions were held, and the city fathers made their decisions.

When the Bible speaks of "her husband is known in the gate," it means that he has a position of authority in the city. He may have been a mayor or a councilman or the city treasurer or city clerk. He was a man of authority in that city. His wife would be in a place of honor in the city because she belonged to him.

This is a little background of what it says in Proverbs about being honored in the gate. Isn't that lovely? Here he is, the mayor of a city. He is at the gate of the city, and his wife shares that position of honor with him.

10. Creation of Man

Was Adam made after the sixth day, and was this another generation? In Genesis 2:7 we read, "And the Lord God formed man of the dust of the ground, and breathed into his nostrils the breath of life . . ."

Mrs. Sugden: In Genesis 1:26 we read, "And God said, Let us make man in our image, after our likeness . . ." Then in verse 27, " . . . in the image of God created He him . . ." then in verse 30, " . . . I have given every green herb for meat . . ." And in verse 31, " . . . And the evening and the morning were the sixth day."

Genesis 2:4 says, "These are the generations of the heavens and the earth when they were created, in the day that the Lord God made the earth and the heavens."

Dr. Sugden: What you have in Genesis chapters 1, 2, and 3 is a general description of the creation followed by another description given in detail. First, God states the fact that He created. Then someone may ask, "How did He do it?" So God has a second chapter. These are not different acts. Chapter 2 is not some appendage. When God said in Genesis 2:7, " . . . and breathed into his nostrils the breath of life; and man became a living soul," He was giving details about what He had done in chapter 1. That verse explains how He made man—how He did it! God frequently did this in the Bible. He stated something, then He went back to recapitulate. He tells us what He had said.

The same thing is true in Genesis 9, 10, and 11. First, God divided the nations. Then He told us how it happened. He could have said it all at once, but He didn't. He went back to explain it. And that is exactly what God did in Genesis chapters 1 and 2. It was not two creative acts. God created, then He explained how He created.

11. Creation (Six Days)

Are the six days of creation 24-hour days as we know them?

Dr. Sugden: This is a question that has divided denominations and has divided God's people. It is terrible to divide yourselves over things like this.

I have a conviction, and since you ask what I think, I will tell you. I believe that the 6 days of Genesis 1 were 6 days. You may disagree with me. You may say, "I think they were 1000-year days." But you have great problems with that. You have grass growing and things existing for a thousand years without any light. You have great problems.

Turn to Exodus 31, which discusses the Sabbath day. This is not a passage that deals with creation, but I think it will help you. We read: "Speak thou also unto the children of Israel, saying,..." What children were they? ISRAEL! Don't forget that. Put a circle around it. I have a host of friends that call themselves Adventists. They have never read this. If they have they close their eyes and mumble. (One of the great ways to misinterpret the Bible is to close your eyes and mumble.)

> "Speak thou also unto the children of Israel, saying, Verily My sabbaths ye shall keep: for it is a sign between Me and you..."
>
> (Exodus 31:13).

God didn't say it is a sign between Him and the church. He didn't say it was a sign between Him and the Gentiles. He said it was a sign between Him and you, and the "you" is "Israel." So the Sabbath was given to Israel.

God gave a sign to the nation and to a people. He did not give it to the Church. Yet we have believers today holding to the Sabbath Day. It isn't for us! We have a day—the day of resurrection, the day Christ rose from the dead, the day the Church was born, the day the early church kept and took up its offerings. Not only does the Word of God tell us this, but history tells us too.

Now back to Exodus 31:16, "Wherefore the children of Israel shall keep the sabbath, to observe the sabbath throughout their generations, for a perpetual covenant."

Now verse 17. This is my argument: "It is a sign between me and the children of Israel forever: for in six days the Lord made heaven and earth...."

Do you know what God is saying? He is saying that the sabbath day is a *day*—not 500 years, or 100 years, or 1000 years. Just think, wouldn't it be great if you could have one Sunday that was a thousand years long! Look how long you could sleep! Or preach! Yes, wouldn't that be something!

Let me repeat, "for in six days the Lord made heaven and

earth, and on the seventh day He rested, and was refreshed''
(Ex. 31:17).

This is my great argument. God said in essence, "As you, the
children of Israel, keep your six days and remember a seventh
day, so the Lord made the heaven and earth in six days and
rested on the seventh day.'' They have 24-hour days in Israel,
just as we have here.

God was saying something here. He was saying that just as
you live and work six days, I made the earth in six days. He
made it in six days, and then He rested on one day.

12. Dispensationalism

What is dispensationalism?

Dr. Sugden: The very moment you pick up your Bible and
open it you become a dispensationalist. This is because the
Bible has two testaments: the Old Testament and the New
Testament. The Old Testament has to do with the dispensation
of law, and the New Testament has to do with the dispensation
of grace.

A dispensation is a period of time in which God deals in a
specific way with people. For instance, in our study of the life
of Abraham, who was he? He was a Hebrew. How did he
happen to be a Hebrew? Where did this happen?

You begin to realize that God did deal with the people at
the time of the flood, and those previous to the flood, in a
particular way.

Then He dealt with people another way after the flood. He
began to call out "a people for His name," Jewish people, the
descendants of Abraham, Isaac, and Jacob. In each of the dispensations, God dealt with people in a special way.

Some say, "Well, if you are a dispensationalist, you don't
believe that God saves people.'' God saves people in the same
manner all the way through every dispensation; that is, they are
saved by faith and by grace.

But the dispensations move along, and then there is a fulness
of time in the plan and program of God, when the Lord Jesus
comes. The old law came to an abrupt end. He nailed it to the
cross and put it away forever.

If people do not understand this, they become confused. For
instance, my Adventist friends do not like me because we insist
that the Word of God teaches that the Old Testament law and

the dispensation of law passed away. I would not dare to say that, if God did not say it.

You see, people are not saved by keeping the law today. They are saved by grace. When you say that, you are a dispensationalist. Every person who believes that the law was dealt with, fulfilled, completed, and set aside in the death of Jesus Christ is a dispensationalist.

Now, he may not believe in seven dispensations, but at least he has two dispensations. If you take the Word of God and divide it, then you become a dispensationalist. "Dispensationalist" is not a bad word, it is a good word.

13. Dog

In Mark 7:25–29 the Syrophenician woman was called a "dog" by the Lord. That seems harsh. Was Christ acting out of character? Please explain.

Dr. Sugden: I don't think our Lord was ever ungracious. The term "dog" that He used was not the alley dogs we think of that people kick around, and that have fleas and ticks.

The dog was someone that was outside. They were Gentiles, and the Jewish people called them "dogs." It was probably not so much a term of hatred, or even a term to put men down, as simply a way of saying that they were not a part of the Jewish fold. That is the way the Lord Jesus used the word "dog." I'm sure He used the terminology that was being used during that day so that they would understand.

14. The Fall of Man

Was the fall of man the fault of man, or was it the woman's? The Bible says that Eve tempted Adam by saying, "Go ahead, the fruit is good to eat." So was it Adam's fault or Eve's?

Mrs. Sugden: I'll answer this one. It was Adam's fault, because we read in the New Testament, "For as in Adam all die . . ." (1 Cor. 15:22). It does not say that "as in Eve all die."

Dr. Sugden: Are you ever good this morning! That is true.

15. God, and Man in God's Image

In Genesis 1:26, when God speaks, who is "our"?

Dr. Sugden: The verse begins, "And God said." Someday, if you want a good time, take a ballpoint pen and go through Genesis 1, and mark all the times, "God said." God is saying things all the time. He just can't stop talking, "And God said," "and God said"—ten times! This is the decalogue of creation. He spoke ten times in this chapter, and in verse 26 of the first chapter of Genesis, this is one of the "God said's."

"And God said, Let us make man in OUR image, after OUR likeness . . . ."

Now the question is, "Who is the Our?" Of course, it is God. Then you ask, "Why doesn't He say, "Let Me make man in My image?" Because God is a tripartite being. He is a trinity in Himself, and so He used the word "our." He says we are going to make man like we are. Now look at what He did, and how He did it. Genesis 1:27 reads, "So God created man in His own image . . . ."

How did He make man? He made man a tripartite being, so that there are three parts to you. You are quite something. Did you know that? He made a spirit, and He made a soul, and He made a body into which He put the spirit and the soul. So there are three parts to you—and three parts to God. Just think! He has emotion, intellect and will. And He gave you emotions, intellect and will. He gave you a body, soul and spirit.

Your *spirit* is the capacity you have for God. Every created person in the world has a God-capacity. This is the wonder of doing personal work, because every person you will ever speak to or deal with has a capacity for God. He might say, "Well, I'm not interested in that at all," but he has a capacity for God. God made him that way. He has a spirit.

What else did God make? He made him a *soul*. You ask, "What does that do?" David said, "Hast thou seen Him whom my soul loves?" So the soul is the seat of my affections. It has to do with my relationship with people. My spirit has to do with my relationship with God. Now my soul has to do with my relationship with people. It is with my soul that I love people. I hope you love people. They are the nicest things God made.

Then my *body* is my earth-consciousness. This is where I live. I am related to earth, and to the magnificense of God's creation. We could spend the rest of our lives in Genesis 1, reading and studying about the body and the soul and the spirit.

16. God's Judgment

In the Book of Joshua, God commanded the Israelites to kill all the men, women, and children in several sites. It is diffi-

cult for me to understand why God would have the children slaughtered.

Dr. Sugden: The reason the children were killed is because children grow up. This was an extreme measure. You see, when the children of Israel marched into the land of Palestine, the Word of God says in Leviticus and Deuteronomy that the people of that land had so corrupted themselves that when they walked across the pasture fields, the grounds looked up and said to the people that walked on them, "You make me sick to my stomach."

The people had gone out after false gods. They had corrupted themselves in all kinds of sin. When God moved in to give that land to Israel, He said, "You are going to have radical surgery." The radical surgery was the removal of the Canaanites and the Jebusites and the Hittites and all the other "ites." Sad as it may seem, it was essential. Otherwise, Israel would never have survived in the land.

17. God's Repentance

If the Scriptures are as balanced as you say, don't passages like Jeremiah 18:9, 10 and 1 Samuel 2:30 temper what Jeremiah 31:35–37 says about the Jews? Hasn't their disobedience forced God to change His mind?

Mrs. Sugden: No!

Dr. Sugden: First of all, look at Jeremiah 18:8–10.

"If that nation, against whom I have pronounced, turn from their evil, I will repent of the evil that I thought to do unto them. And at what instant I shall speak concerning a nation, and concerning a kingdom, to build and to plant it; if it do evil in my sight, that it obey not my voice, then I will repent of the good, wherewith I said I would benefit them."

What does repentance mean when it is God who repents? When we repent, we change our mind about things. But notice, when Jeremiah dealt with this problem, it was the account of Jeremiah going down to the potter's house. How was the pottery broken? It was broken in the hands of the potter. Whenever you hear somebody preach on this verse, you think the potter dropped it. But he didn't drop it. It was marred in his hands. That's what it says. Isn't that amazing? It was marred in his hands. He didn't drop it.

Note verse 6: "O house of Israel, cannot I do with you as this potter? saith the Lord. Behold, as the clay is in the potter's hand, so are ye in mine hand, O house of Israel" (Jeremiah 18:6).

And then notice verses 7 and 8: "At what instant I shall speak concerning a nation, and concerning a kingdom, to pluck up, and to pull down, and to destroy it; if that nation, against whom I have pronounced, turn from their evil, I will repent of the evil that I have thought to do unto them" (Jeremiah 18:7, 8).

What does "repentance" mean here? It is God doing what He said He would do—He is repenting. God said that if a nation repents, I will receive them. When they do as I say, I will keep My word. That's His repentance.

18. God Making Peace and Creating Evil

In Isaiah 45:7 please give the interpretation of the words "I make peace" and especially "I create evil." I know God makes peace, but I can't imagine Him creating evil.

"*I form the light, and create darkness: I make peace, and create evil: I the Lord do all these things*" *(Isaiah 45:7).*

Dr. Sugden: God was not talking here about moral evil. There is a difference between moral evil and the word here, which means "affliction, sorrow, suffering." God will never create moral evil.

That is what James says, and that's what we know about God. But God does allow (and in that sense "creates"—allows) suffering, sorrow, the infirmities of our lives, and our hurts. He allows that, but He does not create moral evil. The moral evils of the world cannot be traced to God.

19. God Winked

In Acts 17:30 we read: "And the times of this ignorance God winked at; but now commandeth all men everywhere to repent."
Please explain what God winked at.

Mrs. Sugden: I was thinking that when you wink, you close your eye for an eighth of a second, but the other eye is open.

Dr. Sugden: Let's look at the context of this verse. We'll go from verse 28 in the chapter: "For in him we live, and move, and have our being; as certain also of your own poets have said,

For we are also his offspring. Forasmuch then as we are the offspring of God . . .'' (Acts 17:28, 29).

We have to watch this verse, because it is quoted by folk who say we are all the children of God. They attempt to prove it here. This does not say that we are all the "children," but the "offspring" of God.

"Forasmuch then as we are the offspring of God, we ought not to think that the Godhead is like unto gold, or silver, or stone, graven by art and man's device" (Acts 17:29).

Paul is talking about the idol worship that went on all through the Old Testament days. It is history. Israel became involved with idolatry, as you know. Now verse 30: "And the times of this ignorance God winked at . . ." (Acts 17:30).

The Greek word translated "winked" is the word "overlooked." God overlooked. What did He overlook? He overlooked their worship of idols. How did He overlook it? By not bringing punishment upon them at that particular time.

20. God's Wrath

What is the "wrath of God" in Romans 1:18 and 5:9?

"For the wrath of God is revealed from heaven against all ungodliness and unrighteousness of men, who hold the truth in unrighteousness" (Romans 1:18).

"Much more then, being now justified by his blood, we shall be saved from wrath through Him" (Romans 5:9).

Dr. Sugden: In Romans 1:18 the word "wrath" is talking about the judgment of God that comes upon nations. Romans 5:9, I'm quite sure, is talking about the wrath that is to come. Paul identified that in 1 Thessalonians 1:9,10 where we read: ". . .who delivered us from the wrath to come." Isn't that amazing! Paul said God delivered us from the wrath to come.

Then in 1 Thessalonians 5, Paul wrote "He [God] hath not appointed us to wrath" (v.9). This is why I'm a pre-tribulationist. The verse in Romans says He has delivered us from the coming wrath or "the wrath to come," and in 1 Thessalonians 5 that "He has not appointed us to wrath."

When I come to the Book of Revelation, I find the church, the body of Christ mentioned nineteen times in the first three chapters. Suddenly in chapter 4 the church is not mentioned again until the 19th chapter. Where did the church go? Where's the church? Well, it's not in chapters 4 through 18.

Mrs. Sugden: Saints are mentioned, but not the church.

21. Gods

In Psalm 138:1, the psalmist stated that he will sing praises to the Lord before the "gods." Who were these gods, and why would he sing before them?

> *"I will praise Thee with my whole heart: before the gods will I sing praise unto thee" (Psalm 138:1).*

Dr. Sugden: The story of history is a story of gods. Sir James Frazer's *Golden Bough* is a ten-volume set on the religions of the world. Someone said there are as many gods in India as there are people, because every person has his own gods. In some instances, there are more gods than there are people in India. There are gods all over the world, and here the psalmist says, "I recognize that people worship all of these false gods."

Our cities are full of cults. So the man of God and the child of God stand in the midst of all of these voices that are saying, "This is the true god." We stand in the midst of it, and we sing our praise and honor to the one true God.

In the psalmist's day there were many gods. The Assyrians had their gods. The Syrians had their gods. They weren't real, but the people bowed down and worshiped them. They had their idols. The psalmist said, I will stand before all their false gods, and sing praise to the one true God. Hallelujah!

22. Humility

Please comment on the word "humble" or "humility." In 2 Chronicles 7:14 the Lord placed humility first in the list of instructions to Solomon as to what the children of Israel must do to receive blessings.

We hear so much today about love, but so little about humility. What is humility? To what group of believers in the local church should it apply? Don't you believe that if it were taught and practiced, it would eliminate many problems in the church today? What is the opposite of humility? Is it pride? How do you think we measure up in this respect today?

> "If my people, which are called by my name, shall humble themselves, and pray, and seek my face, and turn from their wicked ways; then will I hear from heaven, and will forgive their sin, and will heal their land" (2 Chronicles 7:14).

Dr. Sugden: The word "pride," of course, is the opposite of "humility." The word "humility" has an interesting origin. It had to do with a river. When the Nile River was low, and beneath its banks so you couldn't see it, they said the river was "humble." When it overflowed its banks and became a devastating river, they called it "proud."

So the word "humble" means to run low, to stay low. It is the opposite of the big "I" and the important one. I think all the average saint would have to do to be humble is to take a long look at himself. We could never be proud.

Everything we have, we received from God. If we have any gifts, we received them from God. If we have any abilities, we received them from God. The big "I" just does not fit into God's plan.

One of the startling things about humility is that when God speaks of it, He says something important. When you see it the first time, you step back and gasp. The Bible always says, "humble yourself, humble yourself." That is the way the word is used. Of course, we cannot do this without the working of the Holy Spirit of God, but there has to be a willingness in our lives to allow the Spirit of God to give us a right concept of ourselves.

As I recently tuned in to the early morning news, I heard the wildest singer singing the wildest song. It went, "I am important. The only way to the top is to be important." That's the way the world looks on things. But the child of God recognizes that everything he has, he received from God, and he stands with a humble heart.

I believe this is the greatest need in the house of God. Pride is the greatest sin. They say there are three kinds of pride: (1) pride of race, (2) pride of face, and (3) pride of grace. The last is the worst—pride of grace.

23. Jabez

What is the special significance of the pleasant record of Jabez, interjected into a long genealogy in 1 Chronicles 4:9, 10? Why would God want this left on record for us?

"And Jabez was more honorable than his brethren: and his mother called his name Jabez, saying, Because I bare him with sorrow. And Jabez called on the God of Israel, saying, Oh that thou wouldest bless me indeed, and enlarge my coast, and that thine hand might be with me, and that thou wouldest keep me from evil, that it may not grieve me! And God granted him that which he requested" (1 Chronicles 4:9, 10).

Mrs. Sugden: If it hadn't been left in, we wouldn't have known about Jabez.

Dr. Sugden: I'll tell you why it was left in. First, we'll read chapters 1—5, the sons of Esau, Elipas, the sons of so-and-so, and so-and-so, on and on. God says, "Stop it." And He brightens up the landscape and drops this lovely garden of Jabez in the midst of all that ordinary record.

Sometimes God does that. He says, "This is getting monotonous. We have all these people begatting, and begatting, and begatting. We'll change it." So He put Jabez in.

He did the same in Genesis 5. There we have the record, "And he died," "And he died," "And he died," and the Lord said, "That is awfully monotonous." So we read, "Enoch walked with God, and he was not; for God took him." God just brightened up the whole passage that way.

Mrs. Sugden: He did that so we would read the genealogies. Otherwise we might not.

Dr. Sugden: Not many people get a spiritual blessing from reading the genealogies.

Mrs. Sugden: I recently heard a missionary mention that on the mission field genealogies are so important. Some people were saved because of the genealogy of Mary and Joseph in the New Testament.

Dr. Sugden: Oh, the genealogies of Mary and Joseph! If you start on genealogies, you can't just study them for a day. It's a study for years to come.

24. Judas

In Matthew 27:5 we read "Judas hanged himself," but in Acts 1:18 it says, "Judas burst asunder and his bowels gushed out." How do you explain this?

Dr. Sugden: I answer this very simply. If you have ever been in an oriental country, you know it's *hot* there. With the heat and humidity, when Judas hanged himself in recognition of what he had done, his body started to decompose immediately. I believe it decomposed and fell apart, in fulfillment of what God said would happen.

25. Judging

Please explain the words, "judgment begins at the house of God."

"For the time is come that judgment must begin at the house of God: and if it first begin at us, what shall the end be of them that obey not the gospel of God?" (1 Peter 4:17).

Dr. Sugden: This has to do with judging and judgment. God expects that the house of God will be carried on in order. In that order there are certain things we do as believers, and judgment has to begin with us.

If there is no wide moving among our own hearts about right and wrong, truth and error, then we cannot expect God to move. Everything has to start with God's people. It doesn't start out in the world. Revival starts in the church. If there is blessing, it begins in the church. Then, as we are blessed, it spills over to those outside the church.

The same is true with judgment. If God is going to judge the world, He is going to have to judge the world through us. We make proper judgment and proper evaluations, and then they see that God is working in our lives.

26. Judgment of the Nations

You mentioned the ways God brings judgment against nations. Could you list them?

Dr. Sugden: These are some of the forms of divine visitation upon nations. This is not what I say; this is what God says.

1. Famine (Jeremiah 24:10)
2. Storm (Isaiah 29:6)
3. Earthquakes (Isaiah 29:6)
4. Insects (Deuteronomy 28:38)
5. Wild beasts (Ezekiel 14:15)
6. The withholding of goods from a nation (Jeremiah 5:25)
7. Unemployment (Isaiah 19:15)
8. Weak morale (Isaiah 19:8, 9)
9. Loss of freedom (Zechariah 11:6)
10. War (Isaiah 10:5–17)
11. The loss of national position (Jeremiah 48:42)

27. Leviathan

Job spoke about leviathan, a mighty creature. My Bible has it translated as "crocodile" in the margin. I take it that Job was talking about a literal animal. Job 41:13–15 tells of his scales and outer garments and his teeth which make it appear as a crocodile. But verse 12 talks about his mighty limbs. Crocodiles have weak legs. Verse 25 tells that he raises himself up. A crocodile is confined to the ground. Verse 30 says his under-

parts are like sharp potsherds. Then verse 19, about fire coming from his mouth, sounds more to me like a dragon or a dinosaur. "Crocodile" does not fit into it at all. Should I be able to draw my own uneducated conclusion, or ought I believe the creature was a crocodile as the margin of my Bible says.

Dr. Sugden: That's a whale of a subject!

Mrs. Sugden: That question is almost as big as a dinosaur.

Dr. Sugden: I would say that your own uneducated thoughts about this are probably as good as any thoughts you will have. We have to realize that some forms of life have disappeared. Probably some of the life that Job knew disappeared from the earth, so that this may have been a creature Job knew that is extinct today.

But I don't think there is any problem. Sometimes when he describes animals, he speaks figuratively. I think when we read, we have to make our own deductions.

28. Literal or Figurative Interpretation

Premillennialists stress that one should interpret the Scriptures as literally as possible. Yet we see many pictures in the Scriptures. What rules will help in our interpretations? How do we know when to take a portion literally or figuratively?

Dr. Sugden: The context will tell you. When Jesus said, "I am the door," no one needs to wonder whether to take that literally or typically. Jesus said, "I am the door." You don't think He is a wooden door with a piece of glass in it. You know He is speaking figuratively.

Jesus said, "I am the Bread." You don't say, "There is a slice of bread going down the street."

The context makes it clear. Remember, a text out of context is a pretext. That is the way many preachers preach. They pull out a text, explain the text, and forget all about its context. When you take a text out of its context, it becomes a pretext.

Let me help you on this subject of types. When I was a kid, the first group of men I became acquainted with at my house of God helped me a great deal on the study of types.

Look at 1 Corinthians chapter 10. This will settle something for you. As Paul writes in this context, he is reading the history of Israel—the man, the opening of the sea, the quails that came, and the sacrificial system. Now look at verse 11: "Now all these things happened unto them for examples."

The Greek word is *tupos* from which we get our word type. Paul said that everything that happened to the children of Israel happened as a type, a picture.

Now let me give you a couple of illustrations from the gospel of John. Immediately, you will see how wonderful it is. In John 1:47, the Lord Jesus talked to Nathanael, and Nathanael said, "...whence knowest thou me?" (John 1:48). He said, "You knew my name." Jesus said, "Yes, before you were under the fig tree, I knew you." You shall see greater things than these, because you shall see "heaven open, and the angels of God ascending and descending upon the Son of man" (John 1:51).

If you have read the Old Testament text, you would know what the picture was. It was Jacob's ladder (Genesis 28:12). In John 1 you have Jacob's ladder as a picture. But what is it a picture of?

It is a picture of the way of escape that God has made for us. In the New Testament, how is that way of escape? Not a ladder that God drops from heaven, but it is a ladder. He is the Lord Jesus, and He is the way from earth to heaven. The only way that man ever gets from here to there is by a ladder, and he gets there because of Jesus Christ. Now that is one picture in John 1.

Then in chapter 3 of John, there is another way we operate in teaching types. Jesus said to Nicodemus, "As Moses lifted up the serpent in the wilderness..." (John 3:14).

What is He doing? He is taking an Old Testament picture and giving it a New Testament truth. The Old Testament picture "...as Moses lifted up the serpent in the wilderness." The New Testament picture: "even so must the Son of man be lifted up."

In John 6 we read, "Our fathers did eat manna in the desert..." They had manna that fell from heaven and when they saw it they cried out, "What is it?"

In John 6:35, Jesus said, "I am the bread of life." He told Israel, "You ate that bread and died, but I am the Man who has come. I am the manna of God, and if you eat of Me, you will live forever."

Don't miss the wonder of the teaching of types. It is something I enjoy tremendously. When I started out, I overdid it because I enjoyed it so much. I have become a little more balanced now, but every once in a while I just have to preach on types, just to refresh my soul, and say, "This is great truth!"

People don't do this anymore. We are solving problems now,

without realizing that if you take the Word, God will solve the problems.

29. Meditation

Eastern forms of meditation are increasing in popularity. These meditators claim it is an effective drain for stress and a way to achieve a state of bliss or enlightenment. How does the Christian form of meditation compare? What happened in 1 Corinthians 12:2–4? What does it mean to be "in the Spirit" (Revelation 1:10)? How do we meditate? What does one think and feel? What are the benefits? Are the benefits of Christian meditation different than when the Christian studies or hears the Word?

Dr. Sugden: Now, do you want my longest message on that?

Mrs. Sugden: No, No! Make it short.

Dr. Sugden: Look with me at Psalm 1:1, 2: "Blessed is the man that walketh not in the counsel of the ungodly, nor standeth in the way of sinners, nor sitteth in the seat of the scornful. But his delight is in the law of the Lord; and in His law doth he meditate. . . ."

This is a fascinating and intriguing word in Psalm 1. "Meditate" means "to chew the cud." That is almost exactly the Hebrew meaning of the word—to chew the cud. It is a picture of a cow that goes out in the early morning. She says, "Well, the pressure will be on me in the middle of the day, so I'll fill up my stomachs." So she goes along and nibbles the grass and the clover and the alfalfa. When the pressure is on and the sun is hot, she rests under a tree and says to stomach number 1, "Alfalfa, please," and stomach number 1 says, "Here is alfalfa." And she gets that peaceful look on her face and chews the cud. She doesn't worry about being milked that night or being butchered. She just meditates.

Meditation is reflection. It presumes that you already have something on which to reflect. Meditation in Christian thought is usually reflection upon the Word of God. Here is what the text says: ". . . and in his law doth he meditate day and night" (Psalm 1:2).

Then the psalmist gives all the results of meditation: "And he shall be like a tree, planted by the rivers of water. . . ." (Psalm 1:3).

He won't be moved much. "...his leaf also shall not wither..." (Psalm 1:3).

He will be a fruitful man. All these things come out of this art of meditation. It is more than sitting cross-legged.

You may ask, "Don't they find help in meditation?" They find relaxation for their bodies, and probably for their minds, but they know nothing of what we know when we meditate in His Word day and night. Just think, we are planted, and we are fruitful. We go on: "...whatsoever he doeth shall prosper" (Psalm 1:3).

Prospering is another result of meditation.

Mrs. Sugden: I think it is different from studying the Word. It is reflecting on what you have studied.

Dr. Sugden: It is great to meditate—it really is!

30. Nazarene and Nazarite

Is there a difference between a Nazarene and a Nazarite? I know that the Nazarite never cut his hair or drank alcohol. Did Jesus take the oath? Did He drink wine? Where can a complete description of a Nazarene, or is it Nazarite law, be found?

Mrs. Sugden: The Lord Jesus was a Nazarene because He came from Nazareth, but a Nazarite is different.

Dr. Sugden: Turn with me to the Book of Numbers. You should mark this in your Bible. Numbers 6 is a very important section.

The word "Nazarite" is a word that means" to be dedicated," or "to be separated." This is amazing! "Speak unto the children of Israel and say unto them, When either man or woman shall separate themselves to vow a vow of a Nazarite, to separate themselves unto the Lord" (Numbers 6:2).

This was a voluntary step taken in the life of an individual when he became a Nazarite—not a Nazarene, but a Nazarite. "He shall separate himself from wine and strong drink and shall drink no vinegar of wine, or vinegar of strong drink, neither shall he drink any liquor of grapes, nor eat moist grapes or dried. All the days of his separation shall he eat nothing that is made from the vine tree, from the kernels even to the husk" (Numbers 6:3, 4).

It is amazing! "All the days of the vow of his separation there shall no razor come upon his head until the days be fulfilled, in this he separated himself unto the Lord, he shall be holy, and shall let the locks of the hair of his head grow. All the days that he separateth himself unto the Lord he shall come at no dead body'' (Num. 6:5, 6).

Now, think of it. Here was a series of three negatives: no strong drink; no razor; no dead body. This is what is involved in the vow of the Nazarite. You will never drink strong drink; you will never have a razor upon your face or your hair; and you will not touch a dead body.

This is the Word of God. By the way, this is the only place in the Word of God where the life of the Nazarite is set forth.

31. The Ninety-nine Sheep

Who are the ninety-nine sheep in the wilderness mentioned in Luke 15:4? And is the song we sing, "There were ninety and nine that safely lay," scriptural? I heard a Bible teacher say that the ninety and nine were left in the wilderness and were not saved. They referred to the self-righteous Pharisees. How do you answer that?

Dr. Sugden: Note the context: ''Then drew near unto Him all the publicans and sinners for to hear Him'' (Luke 15:1).

So we have a crowd of publicans and sinners who came to hear Jesus. ''And the Pharisees and the scribes murmured, saying, ''This man receiveth sinners, and eateth with them'' (Luke 15:2).

The Pharisees were the critics. Now I think we have to be fair and honest. Sankey wrote and sang, ''The Ninety and Nine,'' and it's here in Luke 15. Yes, there were ninety and nine.

I feel the friend has a point in saying the ninety-nine referred to the self-righteous Pharisees. The Lord was probably speaking in this parable about the Pharisees and scribes. But you have to know that you are lost before you can be found, and one was lost. You have no problem identifying the lost one. The problem is with the ninety and nine.

I would rather think that the ninety-nine were people that were safe. We do wrong when we try to tear the thing to pieces. There are two interpretations, and you can take either one of them and be happy with it. You can say that the ninety-nine were the scribes and Pharisees, or you can say that the ninety-nine were those that were saved and safe. Either way, you will come out at the same point.

32. Old Testament Dietary Laws

Do you think the dietary laws of the Old Testament such as eating pork, apply to us today?

Dr. Sugden: No. Do you remember Peter's vision of the sheet? When it came down, all kinds of beasts were in it. The Lord said to Peter, "Kill and eat," didn't He? There was pork there.

Peter asked the Lord, "You mean I can eat that pork sandwich with mustard? I've never had it so good!"

Now let me say this. I like to think about things. Sometimes I even think about eating. But remember, the Jews were a nomadic people, living out under a hot oriental sun. It was almost impossible to keep meat as we know it today. There was no refrigeration. It was a different set-up. They were nomadic people, but God gave them rules that I think would be profitable for our own health.

33. Other Populated Planets

Does the Bible tell about the other planets? Do you believe that there is life on other planets?

Dr. Sugden: I do not believe that there is life on other planets. You ask, "Why don't you believe that?"

Because of this: Whenever we send a person out to another planet, we take all kinds of time to get little gadgets ready to send up with him, so that he can take care of himself on other planets. The word the psalmist had to say is: "The heaven, even the heavens, are the Lord's; but the earth hath he given to the children of men" (Psalm 115:16).

That does not mean that we will not go out to other planets, but He means (think of it!) the theater of this universe is this earth. It was on this earth that God made man. We can go right to the place, to the Tigris and Euphrates valleys, on the earth that He made man.

It was on the earth that man fell. It was on the stage of this earth that redemption was provided. Not on Mars, or Venus, or Jupiter. It was not wrought out there. It was wrought here! So this earth is the theater of the universe. It is here that the redemptive acts of God are made known. When you read the Word of God, you get to the place where you say, "This is the way it is."

In a university town everybody has his own ideas. When people come to me and say, "Oh, Pastor, you're stupid," I say, "Fine, thank you." But do you know that at this particular moment, the climate among the scientists is this: There is no life on other planets?

It is amazing that at the present time the pendulum is swinging out where we as evangelicals and Bible-believers have stood through the years. There is no other planet, as far as we know, that is populated with people or with some kind of inhabitants or creation. We have no proof at all.

I am excited at what is happening scientifically these days. I read every scientific magazine I can, just to see something about the wonders of creation. The more you read and study, the more you understand that it is impossible for life, as we know it, to be out there.

It was on this earth that God dropped His Son and worked out the majestic, magnificent work of redemption. On a lonely hill, outside a city wall, He died. Not up there, or out there, but here, on this earth! When you get a grasp of this, you get something of what the earth really is.

34. Other Sheep

There are a few Southern Presbyterians attending the services who enjoy your ministry. Do you think that when the Lord spoke of "other sheep that were not of the fold" He was referring to Presbyterians?

Mrs. Sugden: The fold He is talking of in John 10 is the fold of Israel. You know that in heaven there is a river, and when you get there, you can be baptized correctly!

Dr. Sugden: May I say this little word. It may help. Mrs. Sugden and I had the joy of going to college together. She was through when she met me. I took her to another college where she could go through again; where she could teach and put me through.

It was not a Baptist school nor a Presbyterian school. It was a school that stood for the Word of God, for which I am thankful. One of the great points in their teaching was "baptism for the remission of sin." I always have to talk with people about this, because salvation is by the grace of God. We don't add anything to it. They misunderstand the Book of Acts when they take what it says in Acts 2:38, ". . . Repent, and be baptized . . . for the remission of sins." That was said to Israel, and it was not a matter of salvation. It was a matter of Israel, a covenant people, who had sinned and rejected the Messiah. Their baptism would identify them with the Messiah.

We are saved by grace. Presbyterians are saved that way. Methodists are saved that way, and Baptists are saved that way. Salvation is a gift of God. Aren't you glad?

I'm always so grateful to God that so many men have ministered to me. Benjamin Breckenridge Warfield was a Presbyterian; Hodge, a great theologian, was a Presbyterian. Many men have poured their lives into mine, and I'm grateful.

But as Baptists we do stand for particular truths. We stand for them graciously and say, "We believe this is what the Word of God teaches." Aren't you glad we do? If you don't stand for something, you'll fall for everything!

35. Paul and the Book of Hebrews

What makes you believe that Paul wrote the Book of Hebrews?

Dr. Sugden: That's two hours worth of discussion in the classroom! I have always believed that the apostle Paul wrote Hebrews. The indications are that he did.

Peter said that our brother Paul wrote some things that are hard to be understood (2 Peter 3:16). I've always believed that was a reference to the Book of Hebrews, because some things in there are hard to understand.

One of the finest things I ever read on this subject stated that the ancients believed that the epistle to the Hebrews was one of Paul's synagogue addresses. Isn't that something?

I think in recent years there's been a movement toward believing that Paul was the author. Somebody said he thought it was Barnabas, because he was a Levite. Barnabas could have written Hebrews, but I rather think it was Paul.

36. Polygamy

Why does God keep silent in the Old Testament with regard to the polygamy of David and Solomon?

Dr. Sugden: First of all, I go back to this: "Don't read something into it." It is never said that God approved of what Solomon did. It is never said that He approved of what David did. Let's understand first that God does not approve of it. But in that special day, when light had not come to people as it has come to us, many things happened.

Abraham was a man of faith in the Old Testament. What did Abraham do? Well, when Abraham and Sarah didn't have any children, after God had promised them a child, they said, "Let's help God out."

So Abraham took the Egyptian maid to have a little boy so that God would keep His promise. And every problem we have in the Near East today, we have because of that situation that started out with Abraham.

Can't you imagine the birth announcement they would print? God told Hagar her baby would be a wild man. His hand will be against every man, and every man's hand against him.

That was in Abraham's day, and it's as true today as it was then. God does not put His approval on sin. He does not ever approve of sin. He didn't say, "Well, fine, Abraham. You did it, didn't you. You just helped Me out."

No, God came down and said, "Listen Abraham. You got yourself in a bad plight because you followed the flesh." God never approves of sin, but there are situations like some in the Old Testament, when people did not have the light we have today.

37. Prehistoric Creation

We are told by science and fossils that prehistoric creatures lived several million years ago. If they are correct, how and at what period in creation do we tie it in with the book of Genesis?

Dr. Sugden: I have often wondered where they got all these prehistoric animals. They are amazing when they are dug up, but after a while they discover they were not so prehistoric.

Let us suppose that they are. How do we know? Carbon 14 dating is not an exact science—only approximate.

I go back again to say that whatever scientists dig up, whatever proof they have, before all of this took place there was a beginning when God—sovereign, eternal, omnipotent, omniscient, and omnipresent—spoke. Then things were created. If there were dinosaurs, they passed away. They're gone.

Mrs. Sugden: The flood had a lot to do with it.

Dr. Sugden: Pick up John C. Whitcomb's books. He has all the answers in his books. If we believe the Word of God, we have no conflicts, no battles, no struggles with science. In the beginning God was there, and He created all things.

38. Provision for Widows

Please explain 1 Timothy 5:9. "Let not a widow be taken into the number under threescore years old, having been the wife of one man."

Dr. Sugden: In the early apostolic church, they naturally had problems because the Christians were often outcasts. They were pushed out of their jobs. And then there were widows.

Mrs. Sugden: They didn't have social agencies like they have today.

Dr. Sugden: No, they didn't have anything. They didn't get food stamps and all the rest. So the believers took people in. The church became a caring community. They gave to each other. They supported each other. That's the way they did it.

Now, Paul is warning against that. Anyone that is under sixty, he says, ought to be able to work and support himself. Therefore, don't take anyone in under sixty years of age.

That was a good idea, I think. It isn't today, but it was then. The widows had to work then, because that was the way the apostolic church was.

39. Rahab

Why was Rahab blessed for lying? Is this a case of situation ethics?

Dr. Sugden: Do you know Helmut Thielicke, the German theologian? He has written many volumes. He lived during the war. He defied Hitler, and he has many stories about how he got out of situations. Rahab was never commended because she did something crooked. She was commended because she had faith.

Mrs. Sugden: She was commended for hiding the spies.

Dr. Sugden: Yes, for that which was good. She hid them by faith.

Mrs. Sugden: But how could she hide them without lying about it?

Dr. Sugden: She didn't lie when she hid them. She lied when she sent them out. I go back to this— she was not commended because of her deceit. She was commended because of her faith.

40. Respecter of Persons

What does James 2:1 mean when it says, "have not the faith of our Lord Jesus Christ?"

Mrs. Sugden: You have to go on in the passage to get the meaning. You can't take just that much of the verse alone.

Dr. Sugden: The entire verse reads: "My brethren, have not the faith of our Lord Jesus Christ, the Lord of glory, with respect of persons" (James 2:1).

It says "have not the faith of our Lord Jesus Christ *with respect to persons.*" He gave this word to them, and to us, that one of the easiest things to do is to show favoritism to certain people. I have a friend, and the only people he ever sees are rich people.

The Lord teaches against that. This is what He was teaching in James, written to the Jewish people. They were saying, "Well, we will give the best seats to those who are the nice people, and the people who have money."

James said, "Don't you do that." We could label this the "shortsighted usher." The usher says, "Oh, I saw him drive up in his Lincoln Continental." So we gave him a front seat.

Then some little man drives up in his Austin, and the usher says, "There is a back seat here in the corner for you." When people ask me, "What class of people do you have at your church?" I want to give them a good "Mohammed Ali punch." I tell them, "We don't have classes."

41. Rules for Bible Interpretation

How do we interpret Scripture? Are there rules?

Dr. Sugden: I wrote down rules of biblical interpretation in my Bible. I write these in every Bible I own, so I will remember them. They are helpful rules of interpretation of the Word of God.

1. *The Rule of Definition.* How do you interpret the Word of God? The Word of God is written in words, and we have to know definitions. Every Christian becomes a student of the Bible. The moment you are saved, you want to know what the Bible says to you. Somewhere along the line, buy a "word study" book. The best on the New Testament is by Vine. Every

word of the New Testament is there. It gives the English word, and then tells you what the Greek word is. But the definition is in English.

2. *The Rule of Usage.* A Bible dictionary will help you with this, or a commentary on how the word was used in Bible times.

3. *The Rule of Context.* Do not reach in and pull a verse out of context and say, "This is what the Bible teaches." That will slay you. You will find it coming at you in some places where it doesn't say that. Ask yourself first, "What does the context say?" Miles Coverdale said, "Thou must know what goes before and what comes after." That is context. Someone said, "A text out of context is a pretext," and that is true.

4. *The Rule of Historical Background.* If you can find the historical background, it will help to throw light upon a passage. There is an example in the book of Romans. "Therefore if thine enemy hunger, feed him; if he thirst, give him drink: for in so doing thou shalt heap coals of fire on his head" (12:20). I always wondered why it was that if you were kind to someone, you put coals of fire on his head. Isn't that an awful thing to do?

Here is a man who comes to you and says, "Oh, it is so cold in our house, and we need help." He has his little pan on his head, so I heap coals of fire on his head.

I found that this is what they did in those days when fires went out. They didn't have matches or an automatic lighter on the stove. They had to go to their neighbors with a little asbestos plate. It had a thick bottom. The neighbor would put coals in that plate. He would be blessing him. That is what the Bible says. We are to bless them that do evil to us. That is what Paul said in Romans. This is just a little bit of historical background.

5. *The Rule of Logic.* This is a hard rule, and I won't press it because you have to study hermeneutics.

6. *The Rule of Precedent.* Usually words will not contradict themselves in the Word of God. What is used in one place will be used the same way in another.

7. *The Rule of First Reference.* Usually the first time a word is used in the Bible is the key to its meaning all the way through. For instance, not long ago I studied the word "worship." To study the word "worship" as it was used the first time in the Bible in the Old Testament, and the first time in the New Testament, is absolutely amazing.

8. *The Rule of Unity.* What does the Word of God say in its united voice? The best book written on this subject is called, *The Treasury of Scripture Knowledge.* Page 1 in the book is Genesis 1:1. That's the first verse in the Bible, and underneath Genesis 1:1 is listed every verse in the Bible that relates to Genesis 1:1. This book does that with the whole Bible. There is no reading in it. It is just verses, so that there are about 600,000 references.

These are some of the rules that will help you in interpretation.

42. The Serpent

In biblical usage, serpents and snakes are often synonymous with Satan. Of what significance is serpents chasing me in my dreams, or dreams about being surrounded by serpents? Ecclesiastes 10:11 says, "Surely the serpent will bite without enchantment; and a babbler is no better." And yet our Lord in Matthew 10:16 says, ". . . be ye therefore wise as serpents, and harmless as doves." Why "wise as serpents"?

Dr. Sugden: Serpents are smart. That's why they go crawling along, watching for their prey. They don't get up and shout.

One of the things that bugs me about our country is that in the next ten years we will have the most amazing airplanes ever built. They will be run by computer. They won't need a man in them. Just set the computer, and that thing will fly to Russia.

So you know what we do? We tell the Russians all about it. They will be able to get one, and before we have ours completed, they will have theirs finished. We tell everybody what we're doing. It is just so stupid.

Now, snakes don't do that. They don't go along with bells on. The only one that does that is the rattler.

Maybe if you're dreaming about snakes and Satan, you ate the wrong things before going to bed. They tell me that three MacDonald's with mustard will do it for you every time.

You wouldn't believe what I did. I bought a book on dreams. It has 1,000 dreams. You can turn to "snakes" and it tells you what it means. A fellow said he was eating waffles in his dream, and when he woke up the blanket was gone.

Aren't you glad that you can laugh? Aren't you glad you have a sense of humor, and that you can enjoy life and laugh? I don't know whether birds laugh, or cows laugh, or snakes laugh, but laughter is one of the gifts of God to us.

43. The Sons of God

Please comment on the reference in Genesis that the "sons of God married the daughters of men."

Dr. Sugden: This is not an easy question, because there are many varied answers on this. The verse is found in Genesis 6:2, "That the sons of God saw the daughters of men that they were fair; and they took them wives of all which they chose."

The explanation that is easiest to understand does not add problems to your already perplexed mind. In Genesis you have two groups of people, the godly and the ungodly. They are here as always. They are in history. The statement about intermarriage between the sons of God and the daughters of men refers to those who are godly marrying the ungodly. Now, this is the easiest explanation.

Then there are those who teach that the sons of God are a particular group. They were a different kind of being (that is, a supernatural being). They married, which increases great problems about supernatural beings being able to co-habitat with those who are not supernatural beings.

So the simplest explanation, I think, probably satisfies us. If you want to read on this, you can buy books. But I don't think it is a very profitable study.

44. Spiritual Gifts

Do you believe that all of the spiritual gifts listed in 1 Corinthians 12 are applicable today?

Dr. Sugden: Certain gifts were given to the early church, called the signs of an apostle. They were gifts, but they were also signs.

I have strong conviction that when the apostolic age ceased—that is, when the apostles moved off the scene—there were no more apostles. With a cessation of apostolic ministry, there was a cessation of apostolic gifts.

The Word of God not only indicates that, it also indicates that these gifts were given to the apostles as evidence that they were authentic. In other words, they were their credentials. When the apostolic age closed and the Word of God was completed, then these signs and gifts of healing and tongues ceased.

45. Surpassing Power

Would you please explain the "all-surpassing power," as in 2 Corinthians 4:7.

Dr. Sugden: The verse reads, "But we have this treasure in earthen vessels, that the excellency of the power may be of God, and not of us." That all-surpassing power, or as the verse says, "the excellency of the power," is when God takes His truth, His Person, and makes a deposit in your life. He does this when you are saved. It's a jewel in a jar.

Usually we take diamonds and put them in lovely gold settings and say, "Look at this!" The jeweler doesn't put diamonds in plastic, but God does. He says, I take all that I am of My glory, and My power, and I put My glory in a fragile earthenware jar—your body.

The natural man is not naturally kind and gracious, but I have seen the Spirit of God work in a man's life and transform him. You have been transformed, haven't you? But you see, it's not over yet. It is a daily transformation.

The longer we live, the more we become like Him. We look unto Him, and we are changed as we look unto Him. All of the surpassing excellency of His power is in us day by day by day. It is like the word from the sculptor—the more the marble wastes, the more the statue grows. And so the more our lives are tucked away, the more the Lord's life is seen in us.

46. Thomas, the Doubter

Thomas, the doubter is not mentioned often in the Bible. He saw the Lord perform miracles and seemed to be a solid individual. Yet he needed proof. When he was convinced, he became a good follower of Christ. Yet the Christian life is based so much on faith. What do you say to this?

Dr. Sugden: I say just what you said. I have faith in the Word of God. I have faith in God. God is invisible, but I know He is there. I have faith in the Lord Jesus, yet I have never seen Him. I have His Word. I have faith in His Word. I believe in Him. Faith makes Him real to me.

Now, sometimes we need to have assurances. We need to be convinced that this is true. This is why preaching is such a thrill and challenge. Preaching has to be not only dramatic, but sometimes it has to be very dogmatic. We stand up and speak.

When someone asked Joseph Parker, "What shall we preach?" he shouted, "Tell them about God!" They need to know about God, the evidence for God, how we know there is a God. You say, "We know there is a God, because there is a Bible."

You had better start before that, because you have to have evidence. I believe the Bible, and I also believe that I can talk to any university student who will give me twenty minutes and show him there is a God. If he believes in God, then he believes God has a potential of revealing Himself. So the written Word becomes ours.

Doubts are not evidences that you are not saved. Doubts are not evidences that you have no capacity for faith. Doubts are sometimes steppingstones. We make them, and we use them, and they become valuable in our lives. They drive us to study and concern. The result of that doubt, which we want to dispel, is the confidence we receive when we begin to meditate and reflect on God.

47. The Transfiguration

What is the meaning of Luke 9:27? "But I tell you of a truth, there be some standing here, which shall not taste of death, till they see the kingdom of God."

Mrs. Sugden: They saw the kingdom of God in the transfiguration.

Dr. Sugden: Yes, immediately after this, in the gospel of Luke, is the transfiguration scene. I believe this is a picture of the coming kingdom of our Lord and Savior Jesus Christ.

Moses and Elijah were there. Moses had died, and Elijah had been raptured away. Then you have Peter, James, and John, who are alive. They represent the saints who will be alive when the Lord comes.

The whole scene is a miniature picture of what takes place in the kingdom when it is established upon this earth. The Lord will be there in glory. The Jews will be there. The believers will be there. The folk who have died will be there. And those who were raptured, represented in Elijah, will be there.

So the whole picture is a kingdom scene. A few days earlier, the Lord Jesus had said, "Some of you who are here will not die until you have seen the kingdom come."

That day Peter, James, and John saw the miniature kingdom in the transfiguration.

48. The Twenty-four Elders

Who do the twenty-four elders of Revelation 4 and 5 represent?

Dr. Sugden: I have read many commentaries on the book of Revelation to find what these writers believed. I was amazed to learn that the majority thought that the twenty-four elders represented the church.

Then I wrote to Dr. McLain who at that time was still President of Grace Theological Seminary. I said, "Doctor, I need your help. Will you please write to me, succinctly, what you believe about the twenty-four elders in Revelation."

I received a letter, still tucked away in my files, and it said, "Dear Pastor: I have just finished a study on the twenty-four elders, and am convinced that they represent the church of Jesus Christ."

49. The Two Witnesses in Revelation 11:3

I would like your comments on who you think the two witnesses in Revelation 11:3 are. I'm inclined to accept Scofield's suggestion that they are Moses and Elijah, because of what these two men did in the past. But I have read other commentators' suggestions, and I would like to hear what you think.

Dr. Sugden: I too think they are Moses and Elijah.

50. The Unjust Steward

What is the message of Luke 16:8, 9?

"And the lord commended the unjust steward, because he had done wisely: for the children of this world are in their generation wiser than the children of light. And I say unto you, Make to yourselves friends of the mammon of unrighteousness; that, when ye fail, they may receive you into everlasting habitations."

Dr. Sugden: He is stating the absolute truth that the children of this world, the outside, are often wiser in their generation than are the children of light. For instance, consider the way the children of the world prepare for the future. They stack their money in stocks and bonds, and they get ready for what is ahead.

This is a business situation. The man of the world carries on his business wisely. I remember one church we went to as pastor. You had to be a genius to discover what kind of a church it was. I had to pull aside the shrubbery and get down on my knees and crawl to get to the cornerstone. It read, "Such-and-Such Baptist Church."

I said to the men, "Why don't you do something to let the people of the city know we have a church here?"

They said, "They know there's a church here. It's been standing here for sixty years."

I answered, "It certainly has been standing. God knows it hasn't been going."

Then they said, "What do you propose to do?"

I said, "Well, I propose to advertise, because it pays to advertise."

A codfish lays a million eggs, while the lowly hen lays but one.
But the codfish never cackles, to tell us what she had done.
So we shun the codfish, while the hen we praise;
Which only goes to prove that it pays to advertise.

The fact of the case is this: They asked, "How big a sign do you want?"

I said, "I want a sign about 12 by 6."

They said, "You mean 12 inches?"

"No, 12 feet by 6 feet."

"Well," they said, "it is going to be awfully splashy."

I said, "That is what we want. I want the passing crowd to be able to see that there is somebody on this corner doing business for God. I can put out on that sign what I'm going to speak on, and that will startle them. Then I will pray that God will say something to them when they come."

So here was a man doing business. When it all comes out and the story is told, it was simply a matter of business. He said that the children of this generation, out in the world, are often wiser in their dealings than the children of light.

3
BIBLE STUDY HELPS

51. Authors of Study Books

Please give us a list of good, sound authors, such as Joseph Parker.

Dr. Sugden: I just went over books that I have in my library. It's impossible to talk about all the books, but if you are interested in Bible study, you ought to know Alexander Maclaren. His writings are in sets now.

Then get to know Joseph Parker, if only to read his prayers. They are something else. I read them on a Sunday morning often in my study, before the day begins. To read a prayer of Joseph Parker just lifts you out of yourself.

Then I hope you know B.H. Carroll. He had been an infidel, and as a young man he was saved. God worked in his life, and he became one of the greatest students we have ever known. He has an entire set called, *The Interpretation of the English Bible.* He is wild in some areas, so you have to watch him. Don't trust him on Revelation, but in other places he is good.

Then there is J.C. Ryle who was one of the great Britishers who gave us four volumes on the gospels. These notes on the gospels were originally written to be read at breakfast tables of families in Britain. Now pastors buy them, and preach them. They are valuable.

If you are interested in God, and deep things, you ought to know Robert Candlish; and there is Bishop H. C. G. Moule. Anything he writes will bless you.

I hope you know G. Campbell Morgan. I don't know how many volumes he wrote. He was pastor of Westminister Chapel, a great man of God. I suppose that I have 50 or 60 volumes of Morgan. I have most of what he has written.

Another man, not well known, a man by the name of George H. Morrison, was a pastor in Glasgow, Scotland. Pastor Warren Wiersbe and I did a study on George H. Morrison and had it published. As a result, many of his books have been reprinted because of the demand for them. Pastors have found that no one could preach like George H. Morrison.

Another man, not too well known, is F.W. Boreham. He was from Australia, and a great man of God.

Then I have everything that A.C. Gaebelein wrote. You may disagree with him, but don't neglect reading him. This man was ahead of his day. The things he wrote in 1914 are coming to pass now in the 1980's. So somewhere along the line, he was on the ball.

A man by the name of Vine, a Greek student from the British Isles, has given to us Vine's *Word Studies*. Pastors, if you don't have Vine's *Word Studies*, you must get it.

Then the greatest book that has been published recently is *New Wilson's Old Testament Word Studies* by William Wilson. It is an extremely valuable book.

Don't miss A.T. Robertson. He was the leading Greek scholar in the United States, and will stand that way for all time, I am sure. And if you are interested in commentaries, I would encourage you to look at Ellicott. It is probably the best one you can buy today.

Mrs. Sugden: I put down Herbert Lockyer.

Dr. Sugden: Look at his "All" series. He has about 12 volumes on *All the Men of the Bible, All the Women of the Bible, All the Messianic Prophecies of the Bible, All the Prayers of the Bible*, etc.

Mrs. Sugden: Then David Breese's book *Know the Masks of Cults*. And I put down Jack Spark's book entitled *Mindbenders*. I think every young person should read it, because of all the cults in the world today. Young people are faced with them all the time, especially college students. All of these cults get the mind. They're after the mind, to bend it. That book should be in every church library.

Then Guy King has a book for young people entitled, *A Belief That Behaves*, which is a book on James. Dr. Sugden and I like to have all of our young people read that one.

52. Commentaries

Would you list the best small-size commentaries for the first five books of the New Testament, as well as one for the Book of Revelation?

Mrs. Sugden: The Book of Revelation? Wouldn't you need a commentary for the entire New Testament?

Dr. Sugden: Yes.

Mrs. Sugden: *Wycliffe Bible Commentary.*

Dr. Sugden: The best commentary you will have in one volume, is the *Wycliffe Bible Commentary.* For instance, most people do not know this, but Dr. Wilbur Smith wrote the commentary on the Book of Revelation in that commentary, and it is "absolutely fantastic."

It is hard to find a one-volume commentary that will touch all the bases in your study. If I were to live over again, I would build my library around buying books on individual books of the Bible.

Mrs. Sugden: I think that's the best way to study, when you're teaching individual books. I never use commentary sets. I always use individual volumes. I get about five books written about a particular book I might be teaching.

Dr. Sugden: Frequently, I call Bob Kregel, a friend of mine who has a bookstore dealing in used religious and theological books in Grand Rapids. I don't do this anymore, because I got scared out of it once. I used to call and say, "Please send me all the books you have on Jonah." Three days later a truck pulled up in front. It just about scared me to death.

Mrs. Sugden: It wasn't a truckload, though!

53. Devotions

I have a hunger for God's Word, but sometimes find it a chore to do my devotions.

Mrs. Sugden: First of all, have some helps along with you. Do you have "Our Daily Bread" from Radio Bible Class? Use that—it's great! It has the Scripture reference that you are to read with the meditation.

Then you must get Spurgeon's *Morning by Morning,* and *Evening by Evening.* I wouldn't be without that. I read it every day of my life with my devotions. It makes whatever Scripture he has at the top so clear and exciting.

If you're reading just the Bible, perhaps you need a new translation that might be a little more readable. As you read, find out what it says about Christ. Put it down on a paper. Ask yourself, "What does this portion say about Christ?" or "What does this portion teach me that I should do?" Write it down. Look for something as you read the Word. It will help you so much in your devotions.

Then prayer is a part of your devotions. Have a prayer list. Don't just go to prayer and try to think of everything. I have a prayer list for every day of the week. I have it down in a little book. Each day I pray for certain things. Then when requests come in, I add them each day. Do it regularly. It will make your devotions exciting.

54. Family Life

Can you recommend some authors or books that one can trust for sound advice on Christian family life and raising children?

Dr. Sugden: Most of the books written today deal with family experiences, love affairs, break-ups, and break-downs. Not too many theological books are being printed, but there are many books on families. This is where "the shoe pinches" right now.

There's a book entitled *For Families Only* by J. Allen Petersen which answers the tough questions parents ask.

Then Money has a book called *Building Stronger Families*. Bruce Narramore has written *Parenting with Love*. And there is Edith Schaeffer's book, *What Is a Family?"*

There is a ponderous volume, 680 pages, entitled *Parents and Teenagers*. A number of authors have written on specific areas. Pastor Wiersbe has an article in it. I asked him how he felt about this book, and he said he believed it was one of the best he had seen on the total coverage of the family.

55. Helps on Biblical Authority

Please mention book titles that are helpful on biblical authority.

Dr. Sugden: I could list many, but I give to all my young men who are entering the ministry from my church a copy of Edward J. Young's great book, *Thy Word Is Truth*. Nothing has ever been written on the subject to compare with this one volume.

56. Memorization

Could you give us a good method for memorization, or recommend a good book on the subject?

Dr. Sugden: The best way to memorize is to memorize. Don't think about it, read about it, or talk about it, but just do it.

You can buy little cards—I'm sure they're still available—with all the promises of God. Put four or five of these in your pocket, read them during the day, and then start in and memorize.

God has given us a wonderful gift—memory. Use it. I wish I had begun to read the Word of God earlier and memorized it better. I love the parts I've memorized. Memory is a great tool.

And don't confine yourself. Use your memory for other things as well. I have memorized hundreds of hymns. I love hymns and hymnology.

Memory is God's great gift. "And thou shalt remember all the ways which the Lord thy God led thee . . ." (Deut. 8:2).

We have a table that we spread on the Lord's day. We do it in remembrance. Don't forget to remember!

Mrs. Sugden: I often quote to my Sunday school class what the old German scholar said: "The first law of good teaching is repetition. The second law is repetition. And the third law is repetition." This is good for memorization.

57. Numerology

Can you recommend a good book on the study of numerology?

Dr. Sugden: There are two books that I recommend on the study of numbers—not the Book of Numbers, but numbers and their meanings.

First a little book by F.W. Grant. You can pick it up at almost any Christian church bookstore. F.W. Grant was one of the great men among the Plymouth Brethren.

The other is a book by E. W. Bullinger. He has a great book called *Number in Scripture.*

You might find an entry on numbers in a Bible dictionary that tells about numbers and what they mean in the Word of God. For instance, the number 40 is the number of testing—the Lord was tested 40 days; the children of Israel wandered in the wilderness 40 years, and others.

Numbers are meaningful. You should have a book on this subject. The book by Grant is probably the best.

58. Prophecy

Would you recommend Hal Lindsay's books on prophecy, The Late Great Planet Earth and 1980: Countdown to Armageddon?

Dr. Sugden: I have all of Hal Lindsay's books. Yes, I recommend them. I read them.

You might ask, "Is everything he said true?" Everything is true that he said is true. Did you hear about Abraham Lincoln? Somebody asked him to write an introduction to the book he had written. Abraham Lincoln wrote this: "If you like this kind of a book, this is the kind of a book you will like."

Many people have been helped and blessed by Hal Lindsay's books. I just read *Countdown to Armageddon*. It is good, but I don't think it can happen in the 80's. I don't think we should set dates. That is one of the dangers about prophecy.

We believe what God says in His Word. He said that He will come. But we do not know the day nor the hour. But we can discern the times, we can watch, and we ought to be ready. That is the great emphasis.

59. Speed Reading

Do you practice speedreading during your study time?

Dr. Sugden: Yes, I use speedreading, but not the modern method. There weren't any speed readers around back in the days when I went to school. I bought six books on speed reading, and I haven't read them yet.

I'll tell you what happened to me. In college we had a "sour puss" professor in one of our courses. I don't think he was ever happy. It was impossible for him to smile. One day I received a note which said, "Please stop in and see Dr. Lappin."

I went in and said, "How are you, Doctor?"

He said, "Fine." And then he continued, "Sugden, you're not doing too well in class. You can do better, and I think I need to teach you something."

I asked, "What do you want to teach me?"

He said, "I want to teach you how to read. I think you are too slow."

I said, "Tell me how to read."

He said, "You read a page at a glance. I want you to do that. Read a page at a glance, and make a note at the bottom of the page of the most important thing you saw there."

I did that and it picked up my grades. I'll never tell you what I picked it up from, but I picked it up.

Mrs. Sugden: That's the way he reads my notes!

60. Study Habits

Could you tell us a little about your study habits? How do you study the Bible? What do you read for leisure?

Dr. Sugden: First of all, a pastor is called upon to do what his congregation cannot do. Pastors are to feed the flock of God. They care for the flock. One of the cares of the pastor is to feed his flock.

Have a sympathetic heart for your pastor. Study is "blood, sweat, and tears." You need a schedule for your life. I have a schedule. I know what I should do with all the time of my life. I don't divide it up into little 15 or 20 minute segments, but I know what has to be done on Monday, Tuesday, Wednesday, Thursday, Friday, and Saturday, in order that everything will be right on Sunday. I have to do it faithfully before God.

First of all, we use the best Book. I'm to interpret the Word of God for my people, so I need to give myself to the study of it. I have tried faithfully to preach through the Word of God. I believe in biblical exposition. Right now I'm in the Book of Exodus, and I am so excited about it. Every Sunday morning I teach Exodus. In the evenings I usually have themes. Then in prayer meeting we have another Bible study. For all this preparation, a pastor needs an orderly life. Pray for your pastor. My people pray for me, and it's the only way I survive. It is important for a pastor to have good habits in his study life.

Mrs. Sugden: What about leisure? I saw you reading Mark Twain one time for leisure.

Dr. Sugden: I read everything. I need to know what's being said, in order to answer them.

Mrs. Sugden: Someone asked if you ever read books that you disagree with.

Dr. Sugden: Many, many times, because I want to know what's happening. Vance Havner told about the fellow who went lion-hunting and didn't come back. The little newspaper carried a note that said, "Mr. So-and-so went lion-hunting and has not returned. We fear that something he disagreed with ate him."

61. Versions

God has not only inspired (breathed out) His Word, but preserved it. In which translation is the Word of God preserved?

Dr. Sugden: King James! Next question. No, you will not believe this, but I have a good friend who believes that only in the King James do we have the Word of God.

We use the Authorized version, which is the King James version, in our house of God. I had a man leave my church, because he thought I was stupid not to use any other versions.

He didn't know that I had 75 versions on my desk. I use them, but 95 percent of our people use the Authorized version, and it is a great version to read. We read the Word of God together on Lord's day mornings. It is like heaven when we stand up as an exceeding great army and read the Word of God. It reads well. May I suggest that the King James is an excellent version.

Mrs. Sugden: The New King James is good too. Stay with the translations; not paraphrases. That is the important thing. I have read the Bible through in the King James, the New American Standard, and also the New International. I have to admit that I love to read the Bible through in the New International Version. It seems more readable because it is in paragraphs.

I stay with the New American Standard in my teaching. I still like some portions of Scripture in the King James better than the New American Standard. But I stick with the translations rather than paraphrases.

Dr. Sugden: But remember, don't let anyone sell you short on the King James version. Don't do that. All you have to do is buy Cambridge's *History of the English Bible*, and read the account of the translating of the King James version, and study the lives of those men who did that translation. They were no ordinary men. They were geniuses in their own right, and great students of the Word of God.

We have in the King James an excellent version. I think we need to say this, because people get all discouraged when they see so many versions, and they say, "What would you do?"

Mrs. Sugden: I recommend the New Scofield Bible because it has some changes of words that are great. Some of the old archaic words in the King James are hard to understand. And you will be straight on dispensationalism if you have the New Scofield Reference Bible.

4
CHARISMATIC PERPLEXITIES

62. Apostolic Gifts

Some charismatics claim their emphasis in the practice of signs and gifts to be significant because of the approach of a new era; that is, the Second Coming. What do you say?

Dr. Sugden: It would take several hours to talk successfully about the problems of the charismatic position.

You say, "Pastor, you have your prejudices. People are ruled by prejudice, and not by facts."

That is not necessarily so. I believe that as a Christian today, I desire everything God has for me—everything! Now, if God had this for me, then I want it. But I have to know that this is God's plan for me and for the church of this hour.

This has led me, not to some violent 10-minute scan of the charismatic movement, but to spend hours and hours of study. I have read scores and scores of books in favor of it and against it—books on both sides. I have concluded that the gifts given in the apostolic age ceased with the apostles. History says it.

These gifts ceased with the apostles in exact fulfillment of 1 Corinthians 13:8, which says, ". . . whether there be tongues, they shall cease. . ." And they did. Prophecies would fail. There are no prophets today. Prophets belonged to a peculiar age in history, the apostolic age.

The gift of knowledge, in the sense of 1 Corinthians 13, is a knowledge where I could stand up on the platform, look over the congregation, see a man, and say, "This is a child of the devil."

Now, some pastors think they have this gift of knowledge, but they don't. You can't tell. That was a gift of knowledge, and Paul could do it. Paul said to a man who met him one day, "You are a child of the devil." If I ever said that, I'd get a "left hook." We don't do that. These gifts passed away.

Mrs. Sugden: The question is, "Could these signs be significant because of the approach of a new era, the Second Coming?"

Dr. Sugden: No, because there will not be a restoration of the apostles, nor the apostolic gifts and signs. When the millennial day comes and a new day dawns, then we will have all of these glorious things taking place. "Then the eyes of the blind shall be opened, and the ears of the deaf shall be unstopped. Then shall the lame man leap as an hart. . . ." (Isa. 35:6, 7).

When? Then—not now. That's what the prophet says. He didn't say, "*Now* the blind will see."

I have watched this for fifty years. The most deadening thing that happens is to teach that you have gifts. Then parents come, bringing their little babies. They come in blind, and they go out blind; they come in sick, and they go out sick. Then they say, "Well, God doesn't care for us anymore." That is wrong! Do you know what happens to healers?

Mrs. Sugden: They die.

Dr. Sugden: They do. There is a rather thick book entitled, *A Doctor in Search of a Miracle* by Nolan. It is a ponderous book in which he followed up all the healing movements he could. He took down statistics. What he discovered was shocking.

63. Dreams

Do you believe that God still warns believers in dreams?

Dr. Sugden: No, I do not. Hebrews 1 says, "God, who at sundry times and in divers manners spake in time past unto the fathers by the prophets, hath in these last days spoken unto us by His Son. . ." (vv. 1, 2).

God spoke in dreams and in many other ways before Christ came. But He spoke the final word by His Son, Jesus Christ. You don't need any more dreams. Don't get your theology from your dreams.

64. Lifting Up Hands

We would like to know why so many people refuse to lift up holy hands without wrath and doubting. It is instructed many places in the Holy Scriptures, such as 1 Timothy 2:8.

Dr. Sugden: You ask, "Why don't we lift up holy hands?" We do. Every time we pray, we all lift up holy hands. We don't do it physically, but we do it. The writer of Psalm 24 said: "Who shall ascend into the hill of the Lord? or who shall stand in his holy place? He that hath clean hands . . . " (Ps. 24:3, 4).

So when we pray, regardless of our bodily position, we are to lift up clean hands, holy hands, to God.

I shall never forget one of my oldest Jewish friends, now in heaven, Max Reich. One day he said, "Howard, what do you do with your body when you pray?

I said, "Well, tell me, Dr. Reich. You are an old man, and you are smart. Does it make any difference what position your body is in?"

"No," he said, "it doesn't make any difference what position your body is in."

Then I did a little study. I found out that the Bible doesn't say, "Now, if you all kneel, you'll get your answer." It doesn't say that, "because many of them stood, and many fell on their faces, they got their answer."

When you go to the Holy Land or any of these Eastern countries, you see people get down on their knees, and on their hands, and do gyrations as they pray. Do you think God pays attention to their bodily position?

No. The Bible teaches that holy hands are evidence of a clean heart. If you want to lift up holy hands, fine; but God doesn't say that only people who hold up holy hands, physically, will be heard. But in Psalm 24 He does say that you will need to have holy hands to be heard. It reflects the status of your heart.

65. Miracles

Did you say that the miracles done in the Book of Acts were for those in the New Testament days, and not for today? Or did you say they are also for today?

Dr. Sugden: Let me be very careful about this. We have folks come into our church, and then go out and say things we did not say. So once in a while I have to rise up, not to defend myself. I have learned this, never rise up to defend yourself for anything. Anything you want to say about me, I'll never arise to defend myself. God is our defense, and He will take care of things. So I never defend myself.

But I do have to explain the Word of God. So when someone goes out and says, "Well, I was at South Baptist Church on Sunday night, and I heard Pastor Sugden say that God doesn't perform miracles today."

Do you know what that is? That's a lie, because we do believe that God performs miracles today. I'm here because of miracles God performed in my life when I was given up for dead. They told my parents to come and get my body. I'm here, because God was there.

I'm saying that the miracles of the New Testament were the miracles God gave to the apostles to perform as credential signs. How were you to know who the apostles were? By the signs they performed. God never said those signs would continue during this age.

I keep a quiet record, and I know other churches in my city like I know the back of my hand. The death rate in our church is just the same as it is in all the other churches—one apiece. The charismatic churches have as much sickness and as much death as all the other churches have. The churches that have all the healings also have the same deaths.

It is good to look things right square in the face and then find out. Look at 2 Corinthians 12. This is the chapter where Paul asked to be healed, but he didn't get healed. He asked that God would take away the thorn in his flesh. Now, you can't just rub that off and say that it was a mental thing with Paul.

Practically every Bible teacher of any reputation says that it was probably a problem Paul had with his eyes. It was a physical thing that happened to him. Now he asked that it be removed.

God said, "No, I'm not going to do that, Paul. I'm going to do something better for you. I'm going to give you grace to live with what you have." God said, "My grace will be sufficient for you."

So, if you find yourself half-blind, do you know what? His grace will be sufficient for you, if He leaves you that way. Now, God could remove it, but if God does, HE does it. God does not need intermediaries today.

In 2 Corinthians 12:12 Paul said, ". . . truly the signs of an apostle." Do you know what Paul could have said there, that would save me from saying this? He could have said, "the signs of a Christian." But he didn't say that. He could have said, "The signs of a believer were wrought among you." But he didn't say that.

The Word of God is meticulous about what it says. It is careful about what it says. If it were not, you could just add anything to it, or take anything away, and say it wouldn't make any difference what it says.

Paul said, "*The signs of an apostle were wrought among you.*" Why did the apostles have to perform miracles? For credentials. They walked in a world that didn't know them.

The other day a man from the F.B.I. walked in. He flipped open his little leather case with his picture, and said, "I'm from the F.B.I." That was his credential.

When the apostles did a miracle, that was their credentials. It proved they were from God. They had to prove it.

What were the signs of an apostle? ". . . Signs, and wonders, and mighty deeds" (2 Cor. 12:12). God gave the apostles the same power He had. When the apostolic age closed, the apostolic signs ceased. But God's power didn't cease. God's ability to perform miracles didn't cease.

When the apostolic age ceased, the Word of God was completed. So they had the Word of God as their credential. The Jews required a sign. The Jews were still there and in the land, and God was still at work with the Jews, until the time they were driven out.

Three things happened. The Word of God was completed; the apostolic signs ceased; and the Jewish nation was pushed away.

66. Raising the Dead

A short time ago, a TV show told of a Christian who had died in Central China and was brought back to life after the earnest prayers of Christian people. The communists did not believe this happened. At the death of a communist sometime later, these same Christians prayed him back from the dead to prove that God is alive. Is this possible? Are we to believe this? Are all the present-day "miracles" of healing and resurrection of God? Or is it possible some are by the power of Satan?

Dr. Sugden: Let's get the record straight so you won't go out and say something I did not say. First of all, I believe that God can raise anyone from the dead. I believe that! The question is, "Is this the hour in which God is doing it?" Now that is the "sticky wicket." Is this the age in which He is performing miracles to impress people?

In Luke 16 we read that Lazarus went to heaven and the rich man went otherwise. The rich man said, "Oh, if I could just get somebody to go back and tell my brothers. If there was somebody raised from the dead to go back and tell them, they'd believe."

And the answer was, "They have Moses and the prophets. Let them hear them... If they will not hear Moses and the prophets, or the Word of God, neither will they be persuaded if one rises from the dead" (Luke 16:29, 31). That is exactly what the text says. Christ said, "The Word of God is greater than miracles." Now, let's take it from there.

Is this the day when God is performing miracles? Obviously the answer is that for 1900 years God has not been raising the dead. Is this a special thing? Is He raising the dead?

Several years ago, there was a great movement in Indonesia. I know, because we have missionaries in Indonesia. One of the wonders in Indonesia was that they were raising people from the dead. After all this came out, a group of men of reputation went there because they wanted to see it. They searched out these supposed miracles and learned that they had not happened. Several Christian magazines wrote up the report these men brought back — that the stories of resurrection from the dead were not true. There were no people that had died; there were no signed certificates by any physician that death had come. They were people who had been in a coma and who had come out of it. Some people said they had been raised from the dead.

Many false things are going on in the world. I would like to see all these miracles happen, but this is not the day. "Then the eyes of the blind shall be opened" (Isa. 35:6). It doesn't say *now*; it says *then*.

Satan does have power.

Mrs. Sugden: But he doesn't have power to give life.

Dr. Sugden: No, but he is going to perform miracles. So we have to be careful about the miracle aspect. In Acts 2:22, which speaks of the Lord Jesus, Peter said, "A man approved of God by miracles, and wonders, and signs..." These are miracles, wonders, and signs Jesus did while He was here on earth.

The signs of an apostle, Paul said in 2 Corinthians 12, were wrought among you—miracles, wonders and signs—the same three words.

In 2 Thessalonians 2, which talks about the man of sin who will come upon the world scene in a later day in history, we are told he will deceive the people by miracles, wonders, and signs. The same three words are used of the man of sin, the wicked one. When he comes, he will perform the same kind of miracles as the Lord Jesus did, and he will deceive many.

67. Signs and Healing

Please state your explanation of why a large number of churches and pastors do not obey all of the great commission as set out by Jesus in Mark 16:9-19. This passage states that all the signs listed will follow those who believe. Does this include us today?

And what is the scriptural teaching about healing? Are faith healers who hold large meetings and claim large numbers of cures glorifying God? Is this scriptural?

Dr. Sugden: If you have been taught the gospel of Mark, you know there is some question about whether the closing verses of Mark were in the original manuscript. Now, I always give the charismatics their ground. I say, "I will accept that these verses are in the original manuscript," and I use them so. This is the way I do it. Notice what Mark 16:19 says: "After the Lord had spoken unto THEM, He was received up into heaven, and sat on the right hand of God, and THEY went forth." The term "them" and the "they" are the same. Who were the "them" and the "they"? They were the apostles. They went everywhere. The Lord worked with them and confirmed the word with signs. The Bible tells us that "the Jews require a sign" (1 Cor. 1:22).

Remember, now, that the first ten chapters of Acts are Jewish chapters. The Gentiles were brought into the body in Acts 10, and with that beginning the miraculous signs ceased. In the opening chapters of Acts, prison doors popped open, everybody was freed, and great things happened. In the last chapters Paul was in prison.

What is the difference? With the passing of the apostolic age, the apostolic signs ceased. Allow that to sink in! It took a long time for me, because we were cradled in a different kind of theological background when we went to school. They had no definite teaching on this, but I had to have answers. So I bought some good books on the apostolic age—a great age in the church. It was the beginning of the church. And when the apostles moved off the scene, the miraculous ceased.

You may say, "Pastor, do you pray for God to heal people?" Yes, we do pray for God to heal people. I would not spend my days in the hospital praying with people just for the fun of it. I go because I believe God does hear and answer prayer. I believe that God heals. I see it happen, but I am not a healer.

Mrs. Sugden: It doesn't always happen, either.

Dr. Sugden: No, it doesn't always happen. It isn't always God's will to heal. Just think, if it were God's will that we all be well, how many of us there would be on the earth!

Mrs. Sugden: We'd never go to heaven.

Dr. Sugden: We would never die. We would never have the joys of heaven. The only way to get to heaven these days is to die.

68. Speaking in Tongues

If tongues ceased when the apostles died, what are these people doing today who are speaking in so-called tongues? And why are we seeing so many Pentecostal churches springing up, when many other churches that preach the gospel are struggling? Do we not preach enough on the Holy Spirit and the command to be filled with the Spirit?

Dr. Sugden: Let's take the last question first. Just remember this: growth is not always godliness. Every evangelical church should be preaching the gospel, winning souls, and praying. It is the will of God that churches grow, but just because something is big doesn't necessarily make it godly. When we start comparing, we have elements for concern, because we don't know situations.

I have read many books on the charismatic movement. You can't be a pastor today without being interested in the movement. You need to see what's happening, and observe whether it's declining or growing.

To find out all I could, I decided to go to authoritative people who had been a part of the movement and then left. They could give a proper evaluation for me because they knew it personally.

For instance, such a man was Rev. George Gardiner, who pastored the great Calvary Church in Grand Rapids, Michigan, the church Dr. M. R. DeHaan founded. Pastor Gardiner wrote a book called, *The Corinthian Catastrophe*. He had been one of the leaders of the charismatic movement and left because of what he saw.

Remember, tongues in the Scriptures is a known language.

I talked with another man who left the movement. He told me briefly what happens. He said 98 percent of all speaking in tongues is self-hypnosis. That about floored me! Then he went on and said, "There is a certain line you must cross. If you don't cross that line, you'll never speak in tongues. When you cross that line, you do."

Look at 1 Corinthians 14. Remember, this was written to correct the abuse in the church at Corinth; not to encourage, but to correct. Paul said he wanted to correct, so he gave some principles. There are seven principles:

1. The Principle of MATURITY (v. 20): "Brethren, be not children in understanding; howbeit in malice be ye children, but in understanding be men."

This is the principle of maturity—grow up! He said to the Corinthian church, "Why don't you grow up and leave that which belongs to the childhood of Christianity?" This means that when you grow up, you leave childhood. So speaking in tongues was something that would pass. This is the principle of maturity.

2. The Principle of EDIFICATION (v. 26): "How is it then, brethren? when ye come together, every one of you hath a psalm, hath a doctrine, hath a tongue, hath a revelation, hath an interpretation. Let all things be done unto edifying."

Here is the principle of edification. Does this thing I am doing edify? I asked a fellow, "Were you edified?"

He said, "Well, I felt good."

I said, "I didn't ask you that. I feel good when I step out of the ring and have won five rounds boxing with my shadow." I feel good, but that is not the criterion for whether this thing works or not. It is to be a principle of edification.

3. The Principle of NUMBERS (v. 27): "If any man speak in an unknown [unknown is in italics, so it drops out] tongue. If any man speak in a tongue, let it be by two, or at the most by three . . ."

There were never to be over three speaking at a meeting. Here is the principle of numbers. I asked a fellow if they kept that rule in his church. He said, "Of course not. We're always glad to have many."

I said, "God said you can't have over three. Now, who do you think is right, you or God?"

"Well," he said, "I think probably God."

I said, "I think so too."

4. The Principle of INTERPRETATION (v. 27): "If any man speak in an unknown tongue, let it be by two or at the most three, and that by course;. . . ."

"By course"—never together, never two doing it at the same time, nor three doing it at the same time. That kept down the noise and the confusion; and that was the problem in the Corinthian church. He said that you're not to do it that way if it's the real thing. And Paul added, ". . .and let one interpret" (1 Cor. 14:27).

5. The Principle of SILENCE (v. 28): "But if there be no interpreter, let him keep silence in the church. . . ."

This is the principle of silence—no interpreter, no speaking. That's what Paul said. It's very simple. So, if there is a man over here who speaks, there has to be someone who gets up to interpret. If not, no one speaks. These are principles that Paul laid down. I didn't write this.

6. The Principle of CONTROL (v. 32): "And the spirits of the prophets are subject to the prophets."

This is the spirit of control. One of the men I talked with said, "You have to give up control of your spirits in order to accomplish this."

7. The Principle of OBEDIENCE (v. 34): "Let your women keep silent in the churches. . . ."

That is the principle of obedience. Women are not to speak in the meeting. Do you know any place where that principle is kept? I don't. I say to people, "Do you have women who speak in tongues?"

"Oh," they said, "mostly women."

I say, "God says they shouldn't do it at all."

Then somebody reaches in and pulls this out and says that it means you can't teach a Sunday school class, and you can't do anything in the church. This is not what it says. The context is 1 Corinthians 14, which is the context of tongues. A woman has a right to teach, and she has a right to do so many things in the house of God. But a woman was not permitted in the assembly to speak in tongues. This section was written to correct the tongues movement in Corinth.

69. Visions

You alluded to the fact that God does not speak through visions. Please explain. Also, what do you think of the baptism of the Holy Spirit? If the baptism of the Holy Spirit is a gift, how is it that this is not being taught in evangelical churches?

Dr. Sugden: Let me set the record straight. If you are a believer in Jesus Christ, you have been baptized by the Holy Spirit of God. The moment you believe in Jesus Christ, that moment you are baptized into the body of Christ.

In the Old Testament days, God moved, God worked. The Holy Spirit was *upon* men, not *in* them. Then came a new dispensation. God began an entirely new thing in the world.

In the Old Testament days, there were visions. Abraham had a vision. David has a vision. This was the way that God planned it—that they should have visions. Hebrews 1:1 reads: "God, who at sundry times and in divers manners spake in times past unto the fathers by the prophets . . ."

That is the way God spoke to them, in visions. But He is not speaking in visions today. He may get the attention of men by visions, but there are no authoritative visions coming from God today, in the sense of the Old Testament visions.

Why? Because God has begun a new dispensation. In that new dispensation, the first thing that happened was that the Holy Spirit of God, who had been with men, came. On the day of Pentecost, He baptized men into the body of Christ. First Corinthians 12:13 says: "For by one Spirit are we all baptized into one body, whether we be Jews or Gentiles, whether we be bond or free; and have been all made to drink into one Spirit."

So, the baptism of the Holy Spirit is that work done by the Spirit of God when a man believes, which brings him into the body of Christ. When you believe on Jesus Christ, you are baptized by the Holy Spirit of God into that body.

The baptism of the Holy Spirit is not experimental. It happens when you believe in Jesus Christ. The Word of God says it. I am not commanded anywhere in the Word of God to be baptized by the Holy Spirit. I am commanded to be baptized in water, yes; but that is not the baptism of the Spirit.

I am commanded to be *filled* with the Spirit. You see, there is a difference between the baptism and the filling. People confuse the two words. The baptism of the Spirit is for POSITION, and it puts me into the body of Christ.

5
CHRISTIAN LIVING

70. Adversity and Trial

Does God allow bad things to come to us? Does He use them in our lives?

Dr. Sugden: Let us say that God allows bad things to come into our lives and He uses them. If we don't believe that, we're out on a limb if something bad happens. And that's very fragile!

I can say, "Oh, look at the awful thing that's happening to me. How did it happen?" People are always calling the game in the fifth inning, or in the third quarter. People call me and say, "Oh, Pastor, I don't know what's happening to me." I say, "It's not over."

A lady came in the other day and said, "Pastor, what am I going to do with my 16-year-old son? He's never going to amount to anything."

I said, "At sixteen!" We don't call the game in the sixth inning, or in the third quarter. We don't do that. And you don't do that with God. God knows the end. Isn't that great? He tells us not to judge before the end. We're not wise when we do.

I told this mother, "You have been gracious with your child. You have taught him the right way. As far as you know, you led him to Christ. Now let's trust God. You do your best, and then trust God. Don't stand around and 'nit-pick.' Let God have a chance to work in him."

As with the men in the storm in the Book of Acts, God "bringeth them to their desired haven." Aren't you glad He does!

71. Alcoholic Beverages

Will you please comment on the question of drinking alcoholic beverages?

Dr. Sugden: I don't think drinking is a cultural thing. The Bible is not a cultural book. You don't take one section and say, "That's for the culture of this day."

I believe that God is against anything that does harm to this body. That also goes for overeating. Every day I live, I could eat three times as much as I do. I have a friend who does that. You should see him. Overeating doesn't do as much harm as drinking, but it does harm the body.

So God has something to say about excesses in His Word. Proverbs applies to more than the culture of that day. It sets forth principles that are for all time. I believe that.

The Word of God has this to say: "Wine is a mocker, strong drink is raging and whosoever is deceived thereby is not wise" (Prov. 20:1).

Then, Proverbs 23:29 says, "Who hath woe? Who hath sorrow? Who hath contentions? Who hath babbling? Who hath wounds without cause? Who hath redness of eyes?"

Oh, think on these hurts. Who has them? "They that tarry long at the wine; they that go to seek mixed wine. Look not upon the wine when it is red, when it giveth his color in the cup, when it moveth itself aright. At the last it biteth like a serpent, and stingeth like an adder" (Prov. 23:30–32).

Someone says, "You don't mean that's what it does?" But that's what the Bible says!

I work with alcoholics. For six years I was the chaplain in the alcoholic ward. I saw everything. I saw big men, smart men, tall men, little men. I saw ladies and teenagers. I saw everything. I cannot honestly say that wine is a friend to anyone.

Someone says, "Will you not just take a social drink?" Most folks who came through in my study started out with one drink. Most of them never expected they would end up where they did.

I have one more word to say on this subject. Paul wrote this word to Christians specifically: "For meat destroy not the work of God. All things indeed are pure; but it is evil for that man who eateth with offense. It is good neither to eat flesh, nor to drink wine, nor anything whereby thy brother stumbleth, or is offended, or is made weak" (Rom. 14:20, 21).

72. Capital Punishment

Do the verses in Romans 13:1–7 refer to capital punishment?

Dr. Sugden: That section begins, "Let every soul be subject unto the higher powers." Then it talks about resisting the power, and goes on to say, "for he beareth not the sword in vain."

Now, that does not mean that the magistrate goes down the street with a little gold sword on his side and everybody says, "There goes the magistrate."

This refers to the carrying out of the function of government that has to do with punishment; and, of course, capital punishment.

I am quite confident that capital punishment was the original plan and purpose of God. As He talked with man in the beginning and gave him responsibilities, capital punishment was His intention.

But let me say this, that in a day when civilization is crumbling and we wonder what to do; it might be good to go back and have some of the great truths of God incorporated into our system.

Someone said, "Capital punishment will not deter crime." That has not been proven. It has more likely been proven otherwise. I think that it does deter crime, and it is so safeguarded in the Word of God.

God is careful in His Word to guard everything. Capital punishment was only to be carried out when there was absolute proof of the guilt of the party involved. They had to have a certain amount of evidence. If I walked out and destroyed your little girl's life, my life would be forfeited. My life is forfeited by the very nature of that crime. It is what God says, that the magistrate (government) does not bear the sword in vain. It bears the sword to execute authority in the world.

73. Christian Influence

Is today's crisis due to a rise in sin or to a decline in Christian influence?

Dr. Sugden: Both. I think they are inseparable. Whenever righteousness and morality and godliness decline, then sin abounds. This is exactly what we see today. You just can't miss seeing the fulfillment of the Word of God in the events that are happening today.

I read the news magazines. These writers have no idea that they are fulfilling the Word of God; that they are writing about the Word of God being fulfilled. Everything we see today is exactly what Paul said to Timothy: "This know also that in the last days perilous times shall come. For men shall be lovers of their own selves,...lovers of pleasures more than lovers of God" (2 Tim. 3:1, 4)

In this passage Paul gives about eighteen things that men will do. One of them is "without natural affection" (2 Tim. 3:3). Could you say it any better than what the Spirit of God said through Paul about the day in which we live? I think that when morality, decency, and honor decline, then sin abounds.

When Timothy Dwight went to Yale University, there was hardly a Christian testimony on that campus. He purposed that before he left, God would move, in revival. And God moved in revival and changed the course of that university. After Dwight had been there five years, it was hard to find an atheist. So a Christian still can have an influence.

74. Compassion

Is it possible for a layman to cultivate a pastor's heart? If so, how?

Dr. Sugden: When you become a Christian, you are given a heart of compassion for people. That's one of the evidences that we belong to God—a compassion and a love for people. If we don't, we ought to pray that God would breathe compassion into our hearts, because that's what makes a church.

The church is not an organization where people get together for good times. It is a caring organism. In a world of hurts, the church is an oasis. It's a place to which people flee.

I love our house of God, and I love my people. I think they are the greatest people in all the world, and they do love other people. I'm amazed how they love and care for them, and how they do things for each other.

That's the way it should be. The church should be a caring community. We read in the Word how the Lord Jesus moved with compassion, and we too should be moved with compassion. It is not just for the pastor. It's for God's people as well.

75. Critical Christians

Several months ago a non-Christian friend commented that the evangelical Christians seem to be the most critical people. They are ready to criticize anyone and anything, even each other. Why should this be? I have listened carefully for a while since this episode, and I have found much truth in what he said. I now find myself asking the same question, Why should this be so?

Dr. Sugden: There is a spirit of truth in his statement. I have two or three prayers I pray for myself.

First of all, I pray that God will give me the gift of silence. I have never asked for the gift of tongues, but I have asked for the gift of silence. I have enough trouble with one tongue, but oh, the gift of silence! "Lord, give me sense enough to keep my mouth shut." It is a great gift. Sometimes God is a bit slow getting to me on that, but to have quietness is a gift.

There is also a problem of evaluation. I think we have to evaluate what is said, and under what conditions they are said. The Christian finds himself in a strange plight. We stand for truth. If we are believers in the Lord Jesus and have received Christ as our Savior, then we have a responsibility to stand for the truth of God.

It is not always easy to stand for truth graciously. Some of the greatest conflicts I have ever seen have been in the theological world. I have seen men tried for their faith.

I was twenty-two years of age when I saw this man of God on trial, and they tore him to pieces. He stood with grace and courage and kindness. He frustrated the judge with his grace. They asked him, "Do you have a lawyer?"

He said, "I have no lawyer."

They asked, "What do you propose to do?"

He answered, "I will defend myself."

And he did! It was a masterful job. Lucile and I were just beginning our ministry. As I pushed myself farther back against the wall that day, as a young preacher, I said, "Dear Father, is this what I have gotten into in the Christian world? Is this a sample of how they treat men of God? Maybe I really did not hear a call. Maybe I was wrong, if this is the way God's people are treated."

Then I saw the climax of that great day in my life. That man gained stature in my soul, and I thought, *He stood for truth. He stood for God.*

It is not always easy to stand for truth and to stand for God. Sometimes, in the midst of it, we become critical. Paul gave us a wonderful word in Ephesians 4. He said that we ought always to speak the truth in the context of love (v. 15). I believe that. That is my prayer. We have to stand for truth. I refuse to let the cults carry the day.

I think we have a great conflict in our own hearts and lives about truth, love, graciousness, and a critical spirit. It is difficult, but we ought always speak the truth in the context of love and grace and kindness. Maybe we lose the battle, but we lose the battle graciously.

Mrs. Sugden: I didn't know you were going to preach a whole sermon.

Dr. Sugden: Well, I thought I would do it.

Mrs. Sugden: There isn't much left to say.

Dr. Sugden: Go ahead, dear.

Mrs. Sugden: The Bible says: "Judge not, that ye be not judged. For with what judgment ye judge, ye shall be judged; and with what measure ye mete, it shall be measured to you again. And why beholdest thou the mote that is in thy brother's eye?" (Matt. 7:1–3).

It is hard. But if you are perfect, then you can judge other people. But if you are not perfect, you'd better be careful, because they will judge you with the same measure that you judge them. I realize that this is a strong word, but judgment should be left to God entirely. He is trying to make it plain to us that we are not to judge other people.

We can form opinions. We have to do that, because we have to make choices. So we have to form opinions. But I think we should be careful about criticizing other people, because it is impossible to know all there is to know about that other person.

76. Dancing

Should Christians dance? Our son, age eleven, is going to a school where there are school dances. How shall we guide him?

Mrs. Sugden: I would guide an 11-year-old boy into athletics. Encourage him to play baseball.

Dr. Sugden: Sports are wonderful. When we were kids in high school, we had dances and we were invited to attend them. I would rather be with my crowd of fellows in our little boxing stable and have my gloves on. I thought it was much more manly to be in the ring than to be sitting around with somebody, swaying to "Yes, we have no bananas."

Mrs. Sugden: There are so many other good things to get involved in.

77. Death with Dignity

What about death with honor? Do you think it is wrong to request that artificial means be discontinued when all possible measures have been given to the patient, and there is no reason to expect recovery? The Jewish faith takes a very definite stand on this, but our Christian leaders have set very few guidelines for families to follow.

Dr. Sugden: You know, of course, that a local church cannot legislate for its families—only as it teaches the principles of the Word of God. The local church is to set forth the principles of the Word of God, so that people will know how to make decisions.

It is not easy to live today. I believe we ought to have death with dignity. I have a living will with copies given to my family, physician, clergyman, and lawyer. Copies are placed in the hands of your doctor and others so that they have the right, without the danger of being sued, to turn off the machine and let you go to Heaven. It's some day we live in!

78. Gambling

What are the biblical principles in regard to gambling? Isn't the stock market also a form of gambling?

Dr. Sugden: Now let me set this in its proper perspective. When you invest in the stock market, you are not gambling. It's a gamble, but you are not gambling. There's a great difference between a gamble that you take and gambling. A lady in our little store asked me, "Would you like to buy a lottery ticket?"

I said, "You know, really, I've thought about that. Wouldn't it be awful if I bought one ticket and won that million dollars and had my name on the front page the next week?" How would I explain that?

It's like the preacher who went out golfing before he preached on Sunday morning and made a hole-in-one. He couldn't tell a soul.

Gambling becomes as compulsive as drinking, and so we have Gamblers Anonymous in our state. Some people are so compulsive that they will gamble everything they have.

79. Knowing God's Will

Do we really know God's will? Is it the natural man that tells us we can do it our way?

Dr. Sugden: This is so important. There are about fourteen express declarations in the New Testament about the will of God—a framework of the will of God. I can't do anything outside of that framework.

Let me give you an illustration: "In everything give thanks; for this is the will of God . . ." (1 Thess. 5:18). So if I got up this morning and complained about the weather, I was out of the will of God, right? It says I am to give thanks for everything!

Here's another "will of God": "For so is the will of God, that with well doing ye may put to silence the ignorance of foolish men" (1 Peter 2:15). Someone comes along and says, "I don't like you." You just go on and live so well that you will lock his jaws and close his mouth. That's the will of God.

There are about fourteen of these. I don't ever have to ask God about those things in my life, because it is His will. So, instead I can ask Him, "Lord, help me today to keep my mouth shut, because you know how easy it is for me to talk." He says, "Yes, I know that, Howard. I'll take care of you." So He helps me.

Outside the declared will of God, God allows circumstances. He allows things to happen in our lives, in His will. Here's where we have to sort things out. I have a right to say that God has allowed what comes into my life. Then, if He has allowed it, I have to say, "Now I wonder what He has for me in this. Is there some purpose in this for me?"

So He allows me to go to the hospital and have an operation. He allows me the strain of that. But He has a purpose in it. I may not see it on Monday, but I may see it next year.

You have a part in determining God's will for you. God has given you a mind. He has given you understanding. We believe that as Christians, if we desire the will of God, He will watch over us in such a way that we will not make mistakes about His will. We have to make choices. We can't just say, "Well, let God come down and pick it out for me." You can't do that.

God guards us in our choices. If we desire His will, He will not allows us to be out of His will.

80. Lack of Faith

Is God displeased by our lack of faith? Does He get angry by our lack of faith?

Mrs. Sugden: He's displeased I'm sure; but I don't think He gets angry.

Dr. Sugden: No, I don't think He gets angry. But I think that God delights when we trust Him. I think He always puts it positively in the Word of God. He was delighted with Abraham, delighted with Sarah, and he was delighted with men of faith. It delights God when we trust Him. When we just believe Him.

It's hard just to believe God. Somebody said, "You mean you have to believe Him?" Yes, you have to believe Him—trust Him. It's great to trust Him. The greatest days of your life will be the days when you just trust and obey.

81. Movie Attendance

Please comment on Christians attending the theater. And should Christians attend secular theaters to watch Christian movies?

Dr. Sugden: The Word of God says, "Love not the world, neither the things that are in the world. If any man love the world, the love of the Father is not in him" (1 John 2:15).

Then John goes on and describes the world: the lust of the eyes, the lust of the flesh, and the pride of life. These are not of God. They are of this world. The world is passing away, and its lust, but "he that doeth the will of God abideth forever."

We have compounded our problems in this day. We used to have to go to the theater to see a movie, but not any more. We have put the theater in our living room or in our family room.

There are no easy answers. There was a day when we had easy answers, but there are no easy answers today. You don't have to talk about going to the theater. The theater has been brought into your living room. We have to be careful in our selection, and we have to teach our children what is important. We have to set an example and then abide by it.

Then I always wonder why they put Christian films in public theaters. They do in our city all the time, and they invite everybody to come in. Then, as you go in, you see all the things that are going to be shown in the theater in the next weeks.

Mrs. Sugden: The nice part about television is that there is a button. You can even pull the plug.

82. Ouija Board

Our pastor uses the ouija board and plays cards on Saturday nights. Then on Sunday morning he gets up to preach with no power, and to make only a few comments from commentaries. Should I stay there or leave? I teach a class of mentally retarded people.

Mrs. Sugden: I talked to this person earlier, and she said that her young teenagers have already left because they were getting nothing. One of her boys had been turned off because of the life of the pastor. I think she should leave. I know she teaches a class of the mentally retarded, but I think her own family of teenagers is more important. Maybe her class would follow her if she left. Either that, or get rid of the pastor, or pray that he will change. And to spend Saturday night playing cards—I can't believe it, can you?

Dr. Sugden: No, I can't, I can't believe a pastor would use a ouija board, either. That's getting into the occult. I would leave. I wouldn't stand for that. A man named Kurt Koch has many books dealing with the occult. I am amazed that in his experience he figures the ouija board is one of the great problems, and that many times it is satanic—demonic.

No, I think that that pastor needs to be prayed for. If he wants to fool with ouija boards and play cards, maybe he should get a church in Las Vegas.

83. Self-worth

When a child's self-worth is destroyed, can it be restored? And if so, how?

Mrs. Sugden: I think that when a child's self-worth is destroyed, it can be restored if the person who destroyed it is out of the way. But with children it's so wonderful. You can do it by encouraging them. Tell them, "You are something special. God sent Jesus Christ to die for you." Help each child see that he is something special.

I learned years ago when I taught school that you never say to a child, "That is horrible work." You say, "That is good, but I think you can do better." This is so much better to do with children.

You can restore it by having a positive attitude toward that child. That child means much to God and to you.

Dr. Sugden: As a pastor, I have learned that you help people very little by fleecing them. You don't help them by beating them. Before I go into my pulpit, I pray, "Dear Father, help me lift my people Godward. Don't let me abuse them, or hurt or destroy them."

People need to know that they are of tremendous value to God. Do you think He would have sent His Son to pay the price of redemption for you if you were not of value to Him? Of course not! People need to know that they are important to God. They are of tremendous value.

To restore feeling of self-worth is one of the greatest problems we have in our ministry. Many people call me and say, "Pastor, I just feel like I'm nothing anymore." I have to start in and work with them to build them up. I say, "Well, you are something."

The greatest letters I get in my ministry are letters from people who write and say, "Pastor, you lifted me up and picked me up, when I didn't think there was any hope." As Christians, this is what we are to do for one another. We are to be encouragers.

84. Separation

I'm a relatively new Christian and a member of a Baptist church. My own family is non-Christian. My close relatives are in a legalistic church. I have had some Sunday school teaching as a child with my relatives.

Although they accept me as a Christian, they tell me I'm not in the right church. I plan to attend my first year of Bible school in the fall. They do not believe in Bible school. They say it isn't necessary. I know I am to love my relatives as Christian brothers and sisters, but what should my response and attitude be? I want peace in my heart.

Dr. Sugden: Don't let the relatives heckle you! We are not saved by legalism or living by the law. Christianity has been dealt an injustice by legalistic teaching.

You say, "Well then, it is easy to go the other way and be free."

No, it isn't. Not in the light of the Word of God. The Word of God is very careful about our lives.

I have some friends who were legalistic. Their women had to wear a certain garb. If they didn't wear that, they weren't Christians. Where do you find that in the Bible? It doesn't say that women's dresses must always be grey.

One of their pastors asked me to lunch. He said, "I have sensed as I heard you preach, that you have truths that we don't know anything about. What would you do if you were in my place? My great-grandfather was a bishop, and my father is a bishop in this church." And he was the youngest bishop in that church.

He said, "I don't dare to wear a tie, because I'd be criticized. If my wife's little hat gets any smaller, then she is not spiritual."

Dear Christian friends, that is not Christian faith and life. That is an appendage tacked on by men. When we become members of the family of God, we come into a great fellowship—the fellowship of God's family. I think that the Lord delineates for us very well how we are to live. The Bible talks about drinking. Someone says, "You're free to drink, then?"

"No," the Bible says, "You don't drink."

You say, "Horrors, I didn't know that."

Well, that's what it says. It designates these things, but it doesn't make us slaves. We have liberty in the Spirit of God, and the Spirit of God enables us, as He lives in us, to do the things He wants us to do.

Now, regarding what they say to you about school. In my judgment, school is essential for pastors and Christian workers. Did you know that when I was saved and began my ministry, there were men in our state who were doing great jobs for God. They were men who had two years at the Moody Bible Institute in Chicago. There was not a Bible school or seminary or Christian college in the state.

It's a whole different world now. Mrs. Sugden taught one class in which there were twenty-five teachers. It is well to have some training, but training doesn't do it all. But it does help us to be effective workers for the Lord Jesus.

You don't go around saying, "I have a degree, and I'm very important." That is not why you go to school.

May God give you liberty among your people, and may He help you live graciously before them. Don't let them disturb you.

It is easy for pressures from the outside to shape us. But when you become a child of God and you are in His family, how wonderful it is to live for Him without those fences that you have to watch every day. Read Dr. Wiersbe's book on Galatians!

85. Sunday Sports

Our 12-year-old son doesn't go to dances and theaters, but he loves to play hockey. In order to play seriously, he must play some Sunday games. Until now, we have not allowed this, but this prevents him from being on the team with good players. I wonder what our position should be. We would not miss our church services."

Mrs. Sugden: Someone once asked Bobby Richardson, "If

you are such a good Christian, why do you play ball on Sunday?'' He answered, ''So you can watch me on television.''

Dr. Sugden: Now let me say just one little word. Mrs. Sugden and I talk a lot about this, because we have problems too. A pastor told me he had deacons who parked their cars outside their church so the minute the service was over, they could hit the cars and get to Detroit for the Tiger game in the afternoon. I think this is all wrong. I think there is a great deal of difference between a mature man of God and a Christian leader in the church parking his car so that he can get out ahead of the crowd and make his way to Detroit to see the Tigers play.

Now, I am a ball fan. But I think we have to be careful not to let our children have a feeling of contempt for the Lord's day because we do not allow them to enjoy themselves. I think that can become dangerous. They can say, ''You never allowed me to do this.''

My father was very strict about the Lord's day. Sometimes we did get out our ball gloves and play a little catch. I think we all have to keep the Lord's day, but you will have to have some convictions yourselves. I cannot pass on my convictions to you, and it will be hard for you to give your convictions to somebody else. This is a problem that you will have to solve in your own family.

86. Tithing

How much of our income should be tithed? Should the tithe come before the income tax is deducted, or can we tithe our take-home pay?

Dr. Sugden: A fellow said to me, ''Don't you think I should pay all of my expenses and living before I tithe?''

I said, ''Well, you'll end up with God owing you.'' You just can't do it that way.

We preach grace in it's proper context, and we preach tithing in a context. Tithing was before the law. It was long before the Mosaic law. Abraham paid tithes, and he lived under grace and in the days of promise. So I believe that it is proper to teach tithing to our people. We teach them that if a man makes a hundred dollars a week, he gives ten dollars to God. You say, ''You do that?'' Yes, we do.

I am in pastors' meetings, and they jump me because Mrs. Sugden and I not only tithe. We do thrice that. You say, ''Well, you don't have the expenses we have.'' That may be, so again, we do it in the light of God's grace and God's goodness. Giving is something that a man has to answer to God for, but I think the basic gift is the tithe of our income. It's good to know that this is the way God ordered it, and this is what we do. We don't just do this—we have never questioned it.

How can you preach to your people about giving if you, as pastor, don't give? I think the pastor should set the norm for his house of God. Our people don't know what I give. We don't have a little board that says the pastor gave so much, and deacon-So-and-So gave so much. We don't do that. We teach that "freely ye have received, freely give." We give to God.

87. Storehouse Tithing

Many pastors teach storehouse tithing—that the tithe ought to be given in the local church, and that only offerings beyond that should be given elsewhere. What does the Bible teach on this matter?

Dr. Sugden: In Malachi we read, "Bring ye all the tithes into the storehouse. . ." (Mal. 3:10). He's not talking about a granary. In the Old Testament days, the center was a city, a building, a tabernacle, or a temple, and the tithes were brought there.

In the economy of the New Testament there is the church (not the fulfillment of the tabernacle). There is a body of believers. That body of believers, the church, has to be supported. Someone says, "How do you preach the grace of God and teach the law on tithing?"

The fact is that tithing was taught in the Bible years and years before there was a law given on giving. Do you know what Abraham did? He tithed! The writer of Hebrews tells about Levi paying tithes in Abraham (7:9). Tithing is a methodical rule. It is not a rigid rule that the church hangs up and says, "Now you tithe or else you are dismissed from membership." We say, "This is the way God would have us do. We give a tenth to Him."

A man told me that in the depression days in 1929 they were penniless. Then he said they started tithing when they didn't have anything, but tithed what they got from selling apples. He testified, "These were the happiest days of our lives, when we put God in His rightful place in our giving."

If we did that today, the local church would meet all of her responsibilities and the gospel would go to the uttermost parts of the earth.

Be very careful where you send your tithe. Once someone wanted money to build a giant balloon that would reach half way from New York to Philadelphia and print on it "JESUS SAVES." He does save, but He does more by person to person than by hot air in a balloon.

6
CHURCH CONDUCT

88. Altar Calls

I find that the New Testament gives us instruction about the things that are to be done during worship service. The only public identification with Christ that is described in the New Testament is baptism, following repentance of heart. How is it that so many churches tolerate public decisions and altar calls? Paul never seemed to measure his success by the number of decisions he got. Can you imagine Christ waiting for the twelve apostles to come forward?

Mrs. Sugden: Well, I think they did, after He called them.

Dr. Sugden: When a message was given to Israel, God, through His prophets, called for a decision. "Whom will you serve today? Anybody here going to serve Me?" Joshua said, ". . .choose you this day whom ye will serve" (24:15). You have it in 1 Kings 18:21, when Elijah stood up and issued a call and said, ". . .How long halt ye between two opinions? If the Lord be God, follow Him . . .".

I don't think you can go through the Bible and say that God is so passive that if you said, "Yes, I believe," that you should just sit there. We are not saved by coming forward in the house of God, of course. But let me say this: when the Lord Jesus was willing to go openly all the way to Calvary for me, it would seem that it might be a great encouragement to someone else if I made a public stand for Christ. I think you have to.

Romans 10:9 says, "That if thou shalt confess with thy mouth the Lord Jesus, and shalt believe in thine heart that God hath raised Him from the dead, thou shalt be saved." Confession has to take place somewhere, and we do it to give people a chance. An old farmer said, "It just seems that it ain't fair to go fishing if you don't draw them in." It's good when you've preached and given an invitation to at least allow for a decision to be made.

Mrs. Sugden: It is always good, because then you have a chance to talk with them.

Dr. Sugden: We do it in our church for a ministry. We don't do it for people to say that so many came forward on Sunday.

We do it because we give people a chance to receive instruction and help, and to encourage others.

89. Amalgamation

Can it ever be in the will of God for a church that has stopped growing spiritually, is losing families to other churches, and is in financial difficulty to either amalgamate with another church or cease to function?

Dr. Sugden: Situations do arise in cities in these days where communities change, problems arise in areas, and people move out. The church cannot reach the community, they say, because the community is unreachable.

I would say that if a church has opportunities at its door, and if things happened within that prevent them from reaching out, there should be an examination. If I were part of that church family, I would sit down with the people and say to those in authority, "Let's survey this. Is it possible to save this situation?"

Sometimes great things can happen, and God can move. I think it was R.A. Torrey who said that he believed that if there were ten people in any church anywhere, if they were to honestly present themselves before God, the Lord would work.

I would not despair. I would sit down and talk with the leaders and have the leaders answer the question, "What about this?"

If there were another church that was doing a job for God, and if there were a possibility for amalgamating, I do not see how you could say it was contrary to the will of God. I think you would be strengthened by it, and the work and witness would go on.

But I think we would need to consider what was happening. Is there a chance for revival? Is there a chance for blessing?

In the goodness of God, Mrs. Sugden and I went to our first church as kids just starting out. We had no experience. There were seven people at the first service. Three of them were visitors from outside the little town, so we had four people.

You say, "Why didn't you close that day?"

Because we believed that God brought us there. Those four people, all elderly, had the desire to see the work go. We believed that God would make it go, if we would work.

We were there for one purpose: to work. It wasn't going to be a holiday for us. It means "blood and sweat and tears." It was work, day and night. So we started in working seven days a week, which we've continued all our lives. Never have a day off, which is the wrong thing to do. But it's the way I started, because there was no way the Lord's work would go—without work.

I believe the church fails because we lose our vision. We lose our compassion. We lose our interest. If that can be restored, things happen.

I believe that we have to take an inventory of the local church situation and see what God can do. Give God an opportunity to work before you join another group. We will be amazed at what God will do when we allow Him to do it.

90. Church Attendance

What can a pastor do to encourage backsliders to come back, particularly those who have known the Lord for over fifteen years? Sometimes one wonders if these people have really been saved, for they seem to have lost any hunger for God and His Word. And why is it seemingly harder to get people out to church? What can a pastor do or say to encourage church attendance?

Dr. Sugden: First of all, I think that as pastors we have to stress the importance of the local chruch. We have to stress that this church is important in this community. Your presence in the house of God is a witness of the grace of God, the goodness of God, and the government of God. Your witness by being in church is the greatest thing that can happen. The writer of Hebrews said: "Not forsaking the assembling of ourselves together, as the manner of some is; . . . and so much the more, as ye see the [note the next two words] *day approaching*" (Heb. 10:25).

He indicates that as we go into the end of the age, there will be a tendency to minimize the local church. That is happening today.

A fellow said to me, "Do you believe in the local church?"

I believe in the local church because Christ loved the church. If I am a Christian, I'll be in love with what He loves. We ought to teach our people about the wonder of the church.

Then I think we ought to make our church services so vital and so attractive, under the spirit of God's persuasion, that people enjoy coming. Some people say grudgingly, "Church again today." We ought to make our services the very best we can—alive! And by the way, it takes more than the pastor. It also takes the people loving and caring and sharing.

I love the little word in John 12 which says, "...they came not for Jesus' sake only, but that they might see Lazarus also..." (John 12:9). Some people came that morning and said, "Lazarus is going to be there. I want to see Lazarus."

You may say that you thought they all came to see Jesus!

We come to see each other. Don't minimize this. The church is the place of fellowship. It is the center of fellowship. Make your services attractive. Make them different. Make them unusual. Make people feel that when they are there, they are important. Say to them, "You are important to me. Did you know that? We couldn't have had this service without you."

The Lord Jesus makes the church very attractive when He is there, and when He is the center. We worship, we pray, we sing, and we teach the Word of God. And we are not afraid to laugh and cry and hurt in church—and show it—because we are with God's people.

Mrs. Sugden: And pray for your pastor, that he won't be boring.

91. Church Discipline

What do you do when there are charismatics in your church?

Dr. Sugden: First, we take a position. Then we clarify our position. You don't meet error with emotion, or with what you may think. You deal with error by presenting truth. We have the responsibility to teach the Word of God and to make the Word of God clear. We let them know our position.

Then, if they are not happy with that position, they will probably quietly go where they will be happy.

You ask, "Pastor, do you have much problem with this?"

No, really we don't. This is because we declare what we believe and why we believe it.

We have watched Roman Catholic friends come to our house of God. When they hear the gospel the first time, they are disagreeable. They say they will never come back. But they do return, and they are saved, and we are patient with them. They have to grow.

We have Jehovah's Witnesses—not many. They are hard to deal with. But Jehovah's Witnesses have been saved in our church, and they have become faithful people of God.

There rests upon the church of Jesus Christ the awesome responsibility to declare the truth of the Word of God.

92. Church Government

What is the biblical teaching concerning church government? What are elders, and how many should there be?

Dr. Sugden: This issue is of great importance, because the local church is a divine organism dropped in history by a sovereign God. For this age, from the time of Christ's return to heaven and the coming of the Spirit of God until the church is removed. This is the age of the church.

Now, how do we know how to run the church? The work of the church in the world is given in the New Testament. For the local assembly, there are elders and deacons. That is the order: elders and deacons. We have trustees because we have a work that is in the world, that has to relate to government. We have to have a group that will relate to government. Trustees do this.

This will help you to see something of the awesomeness of the church. Look at Acts 20:17. This verse will help you have some concern for your *pastor*. You need to realize that in the position he holds in the church, he has at least a five-fold responsibility. He is first of all an *elder*: "And from Miletus he sent to Ephesus, and called the elders of the church" (Acts 20:17). He called for all the pastors in the city of Ephesus to meet him at the corner of 96th and 400. He said, "I'm going down the highway. I'll be there at a certain hour. All of you come out and meet me." So all of the elders, all the pastors, went out.

Now, when you get them there, you read: "Take heed therefore unto yourselves, and to all the flock, over the which the Holy Ghost hath made you overseers" (Acts 20:28).

An overseer is a bishop. These elders were called bishops. He is also the president of an assembly, so this gives me a position. I could take hours to talk about this because it is so important. This gives me a position in the church of being the presiding officer of the church when it meets in its business affairs and meetings. I am not the chairman of my deacons' board or the chairman of my trustees' board, or any other board. But I am the chairman of my church. When the church meets for business, I preside over those meetings. You ask, "Is that essential?"

It is of utmost importance! "How can you expect me to come

and lead the flock of God, if I do not have a position where I can lead them?''

So I am an elder. I am president of the assembly. I am a bishop. I am the overseer of a working force of people. Notice that another word is used here which tells me what I am. I am an overseer who is called to shepherd; so I am a shepherd. Acts 20:28 says, ''. . . hath made you overseer, to feed the church.''

Three offices in this chapter are held by one person: the elder, the bishop, and the shepherd. They are all one. And then, according to the Word of God, I am also a preacher and a teacher. So I have five offices in the church.

Now, a church will have as many pastors (elders) as they need. In our church we have five at the present time. We are all elders. I happen to be the senior elder. I am older than all the other fellows, but they all have their positions, and they are all elders.

It is not a board of elders. An elder is a pastor. As your church grows, you may want to add an elder. He is designated so by the Word of God. This is still true that there are elders and deacons.

93. Control of Church Board

What happens when the chairman of elders and pastor seem to control the church board?

Dr. Sugden: You don't think a church would do that, do you? You mean politics in churches? I don't believe it!

Mrs. Sugden: Yes, they do appear sometimes.

Dr. Sugden: I know nothing about this, of course, because our situation follows scriptural ways. We have some twenty-five men on our deacons' board, and I make very few demands on them. We have a happy situation. We love each other and care for each other. It does not mean they are "yes" men. But I don't get up and say, "Now this is what we are going to do, and you fellows had all better do it."

Joshua was a leader, but he had to move his people some way. A pastor has to do that. He is the pastor of the church, he is the bishop, and he is the elder. Allegiance and working together is something that is gained. I don't think a pastor ever jumps up and says, "This is what we're going to do."

I have found that if there is something I would like to have done, I suggest it in September. By May somebody comes up with the idea that this is what we ought to do, and it is amazing how well it works out.

You drop the seed. After a while, they have forgotten that you said anything about it. Then somebody says, "Boy, wouldn't it be great to do this!" And they go ahead and do it, and the pastor sits back and says, "Isn't that lovely." That is the way it is supposed to be.

94. Corrective Aspect of Ministry

Do you believe there should be a corrective aspect in our ministry?

Dr. Sugden: Yes. There is a great deal of difference between a "scolding" ministry and an encouraging and corrective ministry. The reading of the Word of God itself in the house of God, and the proclamation of the Word of God, is corrective.

You cannot read and teach the Word of God and not have a corrective effect. This is because almost all of its phases have to do with correction. In fact, Paul tells us in 2 Timothy 3 that the Word of God is given by inspiration of God, and is profitable for doctrine and for correction.

One of the most amazing things I ever read was in the biography of David Livingstone. He wrote about the people in Africa to whom he ministered. He said he had seen African people sit in front of him who had their arms amputated and they'd never wimper. They could have anything done to them physically. "But," he said, "when he read the Word of God to them, they cried out in pain. This is because the Word had gotten to them."

The Word of God corrects us. But it takes exposition and application. Scolding bothers us. That is not the way to build people up. But the Word of God is corrective, it is instructive, and it warns us.

We warn people about the wrath to come. We warn people about the things they can do. I have to talk to my young people about marriage. People come to me and say, "What do you do about this? What about this? Do you allow this kind of marriage?" I have to correct them, and sometimes they think I'm an old monster. I really am not.

When I'm stern and hard, I always explain to them that I am not doing it to hurt them. I want to help them. Never hurt them—help them!

95. Forced Unity

When the elders and pastor of a church try to force or demand unity of the elders and their wives, problems seem to result. I feel unity develops as we labor and work together to reach and strengthen the souls of men. Am I wrong?

Dr. Sugden: No, you are right! I had a pastor friend who took over a new church. His first day there he walked in before his office staff and said, "I demand your support and your allegiance and your faithfulness."

A little lady at the back of her desk stuck her pencil at the back of her ear and said, "Allegiance and support is something you earn, Sir, and you will get it if you gain it."

She was right. Allegiance and support and faith and trust and work is something you gain.

96. Intellectual or Spiritual Ministry

We have a minister who is an intellectual. The ministry is information-rich, but lacks a spiritual dimension. His sermons are illustrated with the sayings of secular philosophers, psychologists, and historians. Many people find this boring, and it does not meet their needs. This is my question: Is it all right to try to correct this situation, and to offer suggestions to this man to improve his ministry? Is the minister above reproach?

Dr. Sugden: First of all, let us commend him for the commendable. I think we ought to be concerned about training and education.

Not long ago I was invited to come with my hood and robe to establish a man in a new chair in a theological seminary. I felt I should do it as a courtesy. This seminary established two men in two different chairs that day. We had the meeting, and then we had a break—a smoke break is what it was.

One of my friends talked with me and said, "What do you think of the man that delivered the lecture—the fellow who was being seated in this chair for teaching?"

I said to him, "What would happen to a young man sitting under that kind of teaching?"

He said, "I don't know, Pastor. That is what will come out of this seminary."

We heard the next one, and it was worse than the first. Then my friend whispered to me, as we left, "When I was beginning my ministry, a great man of God said to me, 'Remember that the intellectual is frequently, if not usually, the enemy of the spiritual'."

I'm not sure this is always true, but there is a danger.

97. Ministry to Ministers

Who ministers to the ministers? As is often the case, it is difficult to minister to your own wife, so who ministers to the minister's wife in times of frustration?

Mrs. Sugden: I think other ministers. Dr. Sugden ministers to other ministers a lot. Monday morning is the day that he ministers. Pastors call him from all over on Monday, and he ministers to other ministers and to ministers' wives.

I think other ministers and ministers' wives help one another. Go to Bible conferences where you will be ministered to. Of course, the best place always is God. You can go right to Him. That is the best place.

Dr. Sugden: But the nice thing is for a pastor to have a friend somewhere along the way. Thirty years ago I was ministering at a conference, and a young man was there by the name of Warren Wiersbe. We thought the same, talked the same, and suddenly we were brought together. We have walked together for these years, and Mrs. Wiersbe has become part of Mrs. Sugden's life. We have travelled together in various countries and we have enjoyed each other. We have a "hot line" to Lincoln, Nebraska, and we usually call to talk to each other once a week.

Make friends who will help you. It is good to have pastoral friends, someone close to you in whom you have confidence. You can tell God everything, but some days you would like to have somebody with skin on, someone you can see.

98. Preaching

Do you find preaching declining in this day?

Dr. Sugden: Preaching is "blood, sweat, and tears." It is the giving of one's self. Pastors who think preaching is a cop-out have missed it by a million miles.

I think there has been a decline in preaching, because we don't have a great number of preachers anymore. We have people who give good advice. We have people who teach and instruct. We have people who do many things. But to be a herald of God is the greatest privilege in all the world.

A herald of God! May I say this to you—if you are a teacher of the Word of God in your local church, you have the highest possible position in the world. Just think, to handle the Word of God and to communicate a life-giving, life-building, life-directing, life-strengthening message to people is the greatest!

All we need for our spiritual lives is found in this Word, and it has to be communicated. It is communicated by teaching and by preaching.

Teaching and preaching are a great deal like food. We have some restaurants where the food is fair. I could take you to another restaurant where the food would be no better, but it is served well. It makes a difference how it is served.

Mrs. Sugden and I were in a swanky place not long ago. That night they served 1100 meals with about 200 waiters. They came in at the critical moment, marched into the dining room, took their stations, and you should have seen them serve.

I thought, "Oh, isn't that like a pastor, a Bible teacher!" He's there on the job, and he's going to serve the meal he has prepared. And preparing is a great art.

Those waiters could have stood there with the towels over their arms and looked nice, but if the food was no good, no one would have come back. But when they brought the food, it matched the surroundings.

It is not easy to take the Word of God and arrange it. It has to be put together.

We are to be communicators of the Word of God. In order to communicate, we have to make the message clear and plain and pertinent to life. Pray for your pastor. It is not easy. It is "blood, sweat, and tears."

99. Pulpit Committee

Is there any scriptural basis for the forming and operation of a pulpit committee?

Dr. Sugden: Yes. It is found in the verse that says, "Let all things be done decently and in order" (1 Cor.14:40). That allows for pulpit committees and all the other committees. It allows for anything that produces order.

If I should leave our church, our deacons will immediately become the pulpit committee. Out of the 24 men they will choose about three, and they will say, "We give you men the responsibility of contacting and getting in touch with potential pastors."

It is great to have a good pulpit committee. And when you choose a pastor, remember that pastors are God's gift to the church. Did you know that? They are.

100. Responsibilities of a Pastor

What are the responsibilities of a pastor?

Dr. Sugden: The pastor has an awesome responsibility. I hope you pray for your pastors. The pastor has a five-fold responsibility. He is a bishop. Then he is an elder. Elders in the Bible were pastors. An elder is one who has the position of presiding over an assembly.

As a *pastor*, I am the president of the assembly of God's people. I am also the *superintendent* of a working force. I am to lead the people in their responsibilities and in their work. That means that a pastor works. Lazy pastors bother me.

Then I am the *preacher*. That is a full-time job. Every year I prepare 156 messages. Someone says, "Don't you have any re-plays?" No re-plays! Now that is work, and as Churchill said, it is "blood, sweat and tears."

The pastor is also a *teacher* of the Word of God. It takes time to study. Study is a great privilege, but it is work. It is time-consuming.

Then he is a *shepherd*. He is a shepherd of the flock of God, and that is a most awesome thing. Do you know what it means? It means that there are nights that you won't sleep. It means that there will be days when you will walk with death. Every day all of my life I walk with death. At least half of the days of my life I spend in the hospital with people—and that is not easy. But we are there by divine appointment. We aren't there because somebody voted us out of another church at the last business meeting. We are there because God dropped us there in His sovereign purpose.

So, pray for your pastor. He has these five grave responsibilities. But we also have great joys. It is a joy to be a pastor and to see babies born into the family of God.

101. Staying in a Roman Catholic Church

Do you think that a Catholic who becomes a Christian can remain in the Catholic church, go to confession, and partici-pate in the mass?

Dr. Sugden: I am very careful about what I say about those of other faiths who disagree with me. I believe that I am right. I have a right to my position, and I take a stand there.

I would like to be gracious and kind to others so that I would not offend anyone. As I see it, we have to allow time for development and growth. I feel that if these come to a personal faith in Jesus Christ, receiving Christ as their Savior, and begin to study the Word of God, there will be a weaning away from those things they have known in the Roman Catholic faith.

Be patient with them. We have many, many people in our church who were former Roman Catholics. They believe in the Lord Jesus. They never hear me get up and denounce and scream and yell about things. But we do assert that there is a faith in the Lord Jesus Christ that gives you a new life, new desires, and a love for the Word of God. As you begin to study, you are weaned away from those other things.

102. Struggle With Inerrancy

Our denomination is struggling with inerrancy. What guidelines does one follow in the local church for determining how long to remain a part of the local fellowship? We are trying to be a positive Christian influence, but we need to be taught the solid Word of God?

Mrs. Sugden: I'd get out mighty quick.

Dr. Sugden: First of all, if you have a man in the pulpit who doubts the truth and veracity of the Word of God, then you have nothing. What can you receive from him? If he does not believe in the inerrancy of the Word of God, why preach? Why say anything? His word is as good as that, you see.

We believe in the absolute inerrancy of the Word of God. We make no apologies. We simply stand up and declare that it is the Word of God. We don't seek to explain away and say, "Well now, this is a place where Paul may have goofed," or "It could have been that Isaiah was wrong."

Whatever I believe is in the Word of God, and it is there because God has been pleased to put it there. It has been handed down to us. I say to our people, "We will now stand and read the Word of God." We believe it is the Word of God—no question marks about it! It has to be that way.

When Harold Lindsell wrote his book on inerrancy of God's Word, he incurred the wrath of many people. When I picked up the first volume, I wrote him a little note and said, "I certainly enjoyed the book on inerrancy. I hope you can stand the flack."

A short time later he wrote back and said, "Thank you for your letter of encouragement. You will never believe what I am going through."

Much of it came from folk who professed to be Christian teachers and leaders. They were criticizing a man for taking a stand, and for declaring that the Word of God is THE WORD of God.

103. Women on the Board of Elders

Should a woman serve on the Board of Elders?

Mrs. Sugden: I take it this is in a church where the name "elders" does not mean pastor.

Dr. Sugden: Many pastors tell me that their "elders" are something like our deacons. Elders are pastors, and no woman can serve as a pastor. Also no woman can serve as a deacon.

Mrs. Sugden: But what if the Lord urges them to do it?

Dr. Sugden: It would be the first time in history that the Lord has ever urged anyone to do that which is contrary to His Word. The battle is on right now in many of the churches. This is a real "sticky wicket." Let me establish something. No woman can be a deacon in a Baptist church, because the Word of God says she can't.

Mrs. Sugden: He has to be a husband of one wife, and it would be pretty hard for a woman to be a husband of one wife.

Dr. Sugden: If God gives a woman a gift of teaching, why shouldn't she use it? She should use it in the local church. No woman is taking a position of authority over a man, unless she has a position of authority as a pastor and as a deacon.

When you teach, you are not usurping authority over a man. The one who usurps authority or takes on authority in the church is a pastor and a deacon. This opens a whole field for teaching for women.

7

CONTEMPORARY ISSUES

104. Abortion

Is abortion always wrong?

Dr. Sugden: The doctor who is here at the camp said he thinks the destruction of life is murder. I agree.

By the way, when the early church met for the first (and I suppose only proper) ecumenical conference, they charted the course for the church through this age. The record is found in Acts 15. They designated how men were saved.

At the beginning of the church age, they said that men are saved through grace by faith, plus nothing. Don't saddle the church now with all the legalism of the Old Testament and destroy it. The Jews couldn't handle it. Why should someone ask the Gentiles to handle it? That was their decision, and that is what the church should preach.

The second thing they discussed was Christian conduct. One of the areas they touched on was that of eating things strangled in blood. When you read this you say, "That's an interesting thing, isn't it?" Did you ever eat anything strangled in blood? We bleed everything we kill to eat.

What were the early Christians saying in this? That blood is sacred, and that life is sacred. We've lost that concept pretty much, so we slaughter people in our country. Every year drunken drivers kill 50,000 people. Why? Because life isn't sacred. So fill up your buggy and fill up yourselves, and get out on the highway and kill teenagers. We kill more teenagers than any other group because life isn't sacred any more.

So when we talk about abortions and similar things, I ponder this. Many times I'm called to the hospital to make a decision whether a baby should live or be allowed to die, because it was born with this or that kind of condition. I have to make a decision, and it is never easy.

But life is sacred. Your life is sacred, and my life is sacred. God says so!

105. Battered Wives

What about wife-abuse, child-abuse, and alcoholism? Would

you counsel an abused person to stay in the home in these cases?

Dr. Sugden: First of all, 1 Corinthians 7 talks about being pleased to dwell together. Any person who practices wife-abuse is certainly not pleased to dwell with her. I think wife-abuse fits into 1 Corinthians 7. They are "not pleased to dwell." Verse 15 says ". . . if the unbelieving depart, let him depart."

A brother or a sister is not under bondage in such cases. The word "bondage" here is not just a word that means she or he is a hostage. It is a technical, legal word of the courts. Paul used it to say that the person who is being abused and mistreated is not under bondage to the abuser.

I say this to pastors, because we are caught in a bad spot today. Regardless of what the pastor advises, he is blamed. So let's just prepare ourselves for it. It no longer bothers me, because I expect to be criticized and blamed.

But I always come back to the same place. I am troubled about the things that trouble you, and the greatest trouble I have is about when did the church of Jesus Christ become involved in marriage? That is the problem.

There is not one word in the Bible that gives a pastor the authority to marry anybody. God's Word has records of marriages, but not marriage ceremonies.

I get the authority to marry anyone from the state. Somewhere along the line, the church reached in and brought it into its responsibilities. We have had problems with it ever since.

106. Chauvinism

Somebody said to me that the Bible is chauvinistic. It says, "He begat, he begat." Why doesn't it say, "She delivered, she delivered"?

Dr. Sugden: The reason is that he begat and she delivered. That's the reason.

Someone gave me a clipping reporting that the Council of Churches is arranging to have a new Bible written which removes everything that makes it chauvinistic. They're going to take out the "hims." God is going to be a "person."

A few years ago, one of the great religious conventions in the state addressed prayer to God as "her" for the first time. It is utterly ridiculous and, may I say, damnable.

Mrs. Sugden: What are these people going to do with the

bride of Christ, because that is a "she" and the church is a "she"?

Dr. Sugden: Oh, they'll figure out something. This is one of the great problems of the present day. Things are all out of order. There was a time when God established an order. We didn't start it. God did.

He made man. And the nicest thing that ever happened was that day when Adam sat there with his clipboard and all the animals passed by. I don't know whether he did it in a day or not, but he went down and catalogued all the animals. Every name that he called them has stayed until today. Just think!

Someone said, "Why do you suppose he called a hippopotamus a hippopotamus?" "Because it looks like a hippopotamus." He classified all the animals.

But then it was all over. As Adam watched, a Mr. and Mrs. Bear and a Mr. and Mrs. Tiger walked by. The Bible says that "for Adam there was no answering voice." That is the Hebrew word—"no answering voice"! There was no one with whom he could talk. No one to remove his loneliness, his hurt. None. God said, "It is not good for man to dwell alone." Not good. He didn't say that about a woman. He said, "It is not good for a man to dwell alone. I will make him a help." We always say "a helpmate," but that is not what the Bible says. He is going to make a help meet for him, and you know what He did? He made you, ladies. Don't let any organization steal that away from you.

107. Contend for the Faith

Do you believe that Christians should "contend for the faith" (Jude 3) and expose the apostasy of the World Council of Churches? Or would it be better to stand aloof and say nothing about it?

Dr. Sugden: In the congregation, I like to hear the Word expounded. I like to hear a positive message from the pulpit. I'm a great believer that the Lord can do with the Word what no controversy and fighting from the pulpit could ever do.

I don't think the pulpit is the right place for controversy. Questions and answers, or letters, are good. When the World Council of Churches was exposed on "60 Minutes" on TV and in the "U.S. News and World Report," people came to me and asked what I thought of it.

Then I had the opportunity to tell them what I believe. These are times, as you expound from the pulpit, that you have the opportunity and privilege to use God's Word to deal with the subject, because He deals with everything.

Sometime, sooner of later, you will stand up and scream— and that is an awful thing to do every Sunday. If you are going to deal with an issue, deal with it and then leave it.

My father was a farmer, and he taught us one lesson early: "Don't poke skunks!"

108. Christian Rock Music

What do you believe regarding the different kinds of rock music? What about Christian rock? Is there such a thing?

Dr. Sugden: Christian rock is like a Christian pick-pocket.

Mrs. Sugden: I don't know why we have to bring the world into everything that we do. Instead of getting as close to the world as possible, we should get as far away as possible.

Dr. Sugden: Worship is involved in ascribing worthiness to God in fitting words and music. It is difficult to see where rock music is fitting in the worship of God. We take a stand on this, and people say nasty things about us. But we just go on.

We ought to train our people to enjoy great music. I'm shocked at what is passed off as music in some churches. It is tragic. All rock music does is glorify the flesh. I can't see where it is a spiritual help to anybody. Most of the music, and even the words, don't say anything, and the beat is so fleshy.

Music is a spiritual ministry, not an entertainment. I can't stand this "rock stuff." I don't care if it does say, "Jesus." You can say that on anything. I even see it on sweatshirts.

I know young people like it. It's hard for our youth today. But Christian rock doesn't give any spiritual depth. As I say, worship is ascribing worthiness to God in fit terms and in fit music. When the music gives you "fits," I don't think it's fit to use.

Next to that, the thing that bugs me is tapes. Every singer has to have a tape background. Sometimes you'd like to hear a human voice. Did you know that the human voice is the greatest instrument that God has ever made? It can soar to heights. It can bring sorrow, gladness and hope. I'm a lover of music, but tapes bother me.

109. Cremation

Should Christians consider cremation? Doesn't Amos 2:1 say that it is a sin to burn the bones of the dead? Apparently this is not considered an honorable thing to do.

Dr. Sugden: Amos 2:1 reads as follows: "Thus saith the Lord; For three transgressions of Moab, and for four, I will not turn away the punishment thereof; because he burned the bones of the king of Edom into lime." The Book of Amos is the only place in the Bible where cremation is mentioned, and it is in an unsatisfactory picture and setting. If you were to take this passage out and say, "Here is one verse that has something to say about it," it would say that cremation was displeasing to God. Otherwise, He would not have written it in His Word.

Now, of course, he was talking about taking the body of the king of another country and destroying his bones that way. There was animosity between them, so this was much more than just the burning.

I am concerned about this, because it is happening in our world today. It is much cheaper to have cremation than to have a burial. You ask, "Pastor, what will happen to the folk that are cremated?" Their bodies will be raised. What will happen to the folk that are in the oceans and the seas? "The sea gave up her dead." Nothing is ever destroyed. It changes form, but is never destroyed.

Mrs. Sugden: Don't cremate me.

Dr. Sugden: Have you ever witnessed a cremation? That cured me. I said to a man, "I am going to wait and see this through. I want to see this cremation because I work with people. I have to enter into their sorrows. I have to know something about their hurts, and they come to me for help." So I have stayed through cremations.

I do not want a cremation for myself or for my loved ones. The apostle Paul made an amazing statement in his prayer for the Thessalonian believers. ". . . and I pray God your whole spirit and soul and body be preserved blameless unto the coming of our Lord Jesus Christ" (1 Thess. 5:23). I have never laid hold and fully comprehended all that this verse means, because I am sure the apostle Paul knew that many of those Thessalonian believers would die. But he was praying that there will be a preservation of spirit, soul, and *body* until the coming of the Lord Jesus.

He tells us that in finality there will be a total resurrection and that we will keep our personalities. Just think! I am going to know you in heaven. I will talk with you in heaven about events on earth, and we will do it in our bodies, with our same spirit and our same soul. Our spirit, soul, and body are preserved until the coming of the Lord Jesus. Therefore, regardless of whatever happens to your body, it will be resurrected. Paul is great on this as the Spirit of God moves him in 1 Corinthians 15. He says your body is like a seed sown, and then it is raised. Look at what he says, ". . . and to every seed his own body" (1 Cor. 15:38).

So every person will have his own body. You will not get mine. In the resurrection we will each have his own body. That is going to be a great and wonderful day, when the resurrection takes place at the coming of the Lord Jesus and the saints will be raised.

God fashioned my body. My body is important to God. Think of it! He thought enough of me to redeem me, and included in that redemption was the redemption of the body. That's what Paul talks about in Romans 8, so this body has special significance to God.

Dr. Harry Ironside made an observation in one of his books that I have tucked away in my mind. He felt that God in a special way watches over our bodies as believers, even after our bodies have been placed in the grave.

I know that many have been lost at sea, or burned in fires and other tragedies. But God will not lose one of those bodies. He will raise those bodies.

When you read in Revelation concerning the wicked, "And I saw the dead, small and great, stand before God; . . . And the sea gave up the dead which were in it . . ." (Rev. 20:12, 13). How much more is this true of the saved! All the dead will be raised, but believers will be raised with a special body, a new body, this body—sown and raised.

Amos 2:1 is the only place where anything is said about this. I think you have to make a decision in your own life about it. Personally, I think our bodies are important to God. Therefore, I want my body to be tucked away in the lap of God's creation until He calls me forth.

110. Fundamentalism

What would you say is the difference between evangelical-ism and fundamentalism?

Dr. Sugden: I think they are twins. "Fundamentalism" is not a bad word. We twist words, and we make them nasty or nice. You can do anything with words.

When fundamentalism had its birth, probably 1910, 1911 or 1912, two wealthy men decided to print a series of booklets on the fundamentals. They were called *The Fundamentals*. There were twelve volumes in paperback. Every great theologian of the day addressed himself to some aspect of biblical teaching in these booklets.

These booklets were sent by these wealthy men to every Christian leader and teacher in the United States. Every person got one, whether his name was linked with any church or not. I was not around then, but I have copies of those original books.

They took up everything from the creation, virgin birth, right on through, and covered every aspect. It was out of this that the fundamentalists got their name. It was a great name used for those who simply stand for the great truths of the Word of God.

In the passing of years, there have been extremists. Charismatics are called fundamentalists. There will always be extremists in any movement, and so sometimes the word fundamentalist has come into disrepute. So another word has been given. So we call ourselves "evangelicals." That really means the same thing. I believe that evangelicalism and fundamentalism are closely linked in their thinking.

Both adhere to the great truths of the Word of God. I am not ashamed to be called a fundamentalist. The original two words were good words.

111. Home Teaching

Some people have begun teaching their children at home rather than sending them to school. What do you think about this idea?

Mrs. Sugden: I don't like it. I know that some missionaries have done a great job teaching their children on the field, when they didn't have any other way to teach the children. Now they have schools on the mission field, so they don't have to teach them at home.

When you teach your children at home, there is the danger that they won' t adjust to the outside world. They will have to face it some time, so I think there's a danger in teaching them in the home. I don't like it.

Dr. Sugden: In the United States we use the words "accelerated education." That's where you build a little booth, set the child in the booth, and he sits there and looks at three walls with a tape recorder. He pushes a button, and the tape recorder teaches him. It's something else.

You say, "You're kidding." No, I'm not.

Wouldn't it be great, five or ten years later to say, "I would like to have you come over and meet my tape recorder. She was a great teacher." Wouldn't that be awful!

Teaching is more than just saying things. It's a personality. It's a life. I am glad that God gave me great teachers who moved me, inspired me. They were more than teachers. There was a personality involved.

Mrs. Sugden: I had a school teacher who influenced my life more than any other person, including preachers (that was before I met my husband). It was in a country school. She was a marvelous teacher and a Christian. I wanted to be a schoolteacher because of that teacher. She had a great influence on me.

112. Homosexuality

Recently our Board of Education voted in favor of setting up a committee to prepare information on homosexuality to present at sex education classes in the public school system. What should Christians do about this? Should they protest? Should they remove their children to Christian schools? Or should they quietly pray about it?

Mrs. Sugden: I think they should do more than pray, but they should pray first.

Dr. Sugden: I believe government is given of God, so we do not get involved in government and politics. But when something like this happens in your city, where once again they are attacking the mind by dropping seed into the minds of boys and girls and young people that will arouse curiosity, I would either petition or write.

We write. It is amazing what happens in our country when we write. When one of our politicians gets five thousand letters, he begins to change his mind. When school boards get letters, they begin to get the message. I dare say that in your city, if the people of God were to rise up and write, and speak their piece, they would change the whole thing.

Mrs. Sugden: It would depend on what they were saying

about it, wouldn't it? And what they were teaching about it. I do think our children should be informed.

Dr. Sugden: It depends in part on the age of the children.

Mrs. Sugden: Yes, the parents should know what their children are being taught.

Dr. Sugden: Some of these things the boys and girls should learn from moms and dads.

Mrs. Sugden: Of course. That is the reason Christian schools are being started. Many other things are taught and done in our public schools that are contrary to Christian principles.

Dr. Sugden: We live in a disturbing day.

Mrs. Sugden: But we live in a democratic country. We can voice our convictions, and we do wrong if we do not express how we feel. Parents should take part in the parent/teacher meetings.

Dr. Sugden: Attend your P.T.A. and raise your voice. I remember years ago, when I was a pastor in another city, some scandalous things were being done. It was brought to my attention. I just simply announced in our church ad that I was going to attack this thing on Sunday night. You know what happened? The newspapers sent their reporters over.

Men who had been at some of the meetings where these things were taking place had given me a blow-by-blow description. When I walked into the pulpit, I had Scripture to back me about how God orders lives and morality. I addressed myself to that. They published it in the paper, and so we got good coverage on the issue.

113. Live-ins

What should be our attitude toward those who choose to live with a member of the opposite sex without benefit of marriage? How can we as parents help?

Dr. Sugden: This is the way of life today. But I cannot stick my head in the sand and say, "Well, I wish it didn't happen." Young people come in to talk with me, and they are as open as they can be.

A professor called me recently and said, "Pastor Sugden, if I bring a girl by, could you pound some sense into her thick skull?"

She came in and sat down. She had lived with four different men, and she had a baby with one of them.

The professor said the reason he was concerned about her was because she is so brilliant and has so much to offer. But now she was starting her fifth unmarried relationship.

She told me a little about her life. Then I told her that she should be married if she is going to live with a man. She said to me, with a smirk on her face, "Oh, you're an old fossil. You believe that that little 8 1/2 by 11 sheet of paper that you sign marries me."

I said, "You'd better believe it."

She said, "Why."

I said, "Because of where it came from."

She asked, "Where did it come from?"

"From God," I said.

She said, "You mean that that little sheet that says, 'license' at the top comes from God?"

I said, "Yes, and you will never be married in God's sight, regardless of how you rationalize it, until you have that."

She said, "I don't follow you."

I said, "Government is ordained of God, and the government issues the license, so it comes from God."

When I talk with people, I explain to them that they are rebelling against authority, they are rebelling against government, and they are basically rebelling against God.

That girl has something wrong with her. She is insecure. She is battling. She hates her parents. I have kids come in and say, "Pastor, I did this. Why should I love anybody when no one has ever loved me?" Somewhere along the line we have to stop this vicious circle and say, "Hold it!"

And who can do it better than one who knows Christ and has the love of Christ in his heart? The Spirit of God makes an overflow of that love out to people. So you slip alongside that girl. You know what she is doing. You know she is bad. You know she is living in sin. But you put your arm around her and say, "I'm awfully glad to see you today, dear." She'd say, "What did you say?" You answer, "I'm glad to see you. Did you know I care for you."

You say, "If I said that, I'd be lying."

Well, clear it up and change your attitude. Let God flow through you to some of the people who are unwanted. You learn that the majority of these folk are unwanted, and that is where the church comes in. It shows them the love of Christ.

Mrs. Sugden: Usually it is a spiritual condition. We have had people who lived together without marriage, but when they got saved, they got married.

114. Suffering of Animals

What about the suffering of animals and the present-day use of monkeys for experimentation by doctors?

Dr. Sugden: When I became a pastor, I had to deal with the problems of pain and suffering. I came across a statement I had read hundreds of times, but I had never thought anything about it until then. It is in 2 Peter 2:12, "But these, [Peter had been talking about certain kinds of people] as natural brute beasts..." and here he gathers together all the animals—horses and cattle and pigs and lambs and sheep and all the others—they are "...made to be taken and destroyed" (2 Peter 2:12). That is an amazing statement. He says that God put them in His creation to be taken and destroyed.

Do some study on the problem of pain in animals. I would encourage you to get C. S. Lewis's book entitled, *The Problem of Pain*. It has a chapter on the suffering of animals that is worth reading.

Doctors agree that there is a difference between the nervous system of an animal and that of man. Their tolerance of pain is entirely different from ours.

115. The Shroud of Turin

What should our attitude be towards the possible authenticity of the Shroud of Turin?

Dr. Sugden: To claim it is the burial shroud of Christ is a sheer, thin fabrication. Suppose they did find it was—what would it mean? Our faith does not rest in relics. I am a student of archeology. I love to think of them digging up wonderful things here and there.

Mrs. Sugden and I have stood beside some of those excavations, but whether they find something or don't find something does not change my faith one bit.

"My faith has found a resting place, not in device or creed."

My faith rests in the Word of God, and the Shroud of Turin will not mean one thing to me. It doesn't make a bit of difference. I'll tell you what it makes—it makes for tourism!

116. Test-tube Babies

What should we think about genetic engineering and test-tube babies, when the parents provide the egg and the sperm?

Dr. Sugden: I should have my doctors come up and have a panel. We have lived through this in our city. We have had test-tube babies. We have had law suits and counter-suits. You can't believe what is happening in this situation. Whose baby is it?

I think (and you may disagree with me), but I think it is wrong when we begin to enter into a field that belongs to God. The giving of life, the beginning of life, and all that is connected with life—all of its beauty and wonder—is in God's hands. It is not in the hands of some man with a pliers or test tubes in his hand.

It is dangerous to try to play God. Life belongs with God, not in the hands of men. That is my theme when it comes to conception and babies.

117. Underground Evangelism

What is your viewpoint regarding organizations such as Underground Evangelism? I want to help Christians under communism, and as a steward of God's money wish to spend it wisely. My hope is that most of it will go directly for what these people need.

Dr. Sugden: I wish you hadn't asked that, because this is not an easy question. I identify with God's smuggler. I identify with everything we are trying to do to get Bibles to communists. But I always wonder if we dare to use devious means to promote the work of God. Sometimes this bothers me. I don't know.

Can I be crooked in order to help people go straight? This is not an easy question. If you read Christian periodicals, this is one of the oft-discussed questions. Things are getting brittle, and I praise God for all the times we have had the opportunity to get a Bible into a communist country. I think we should take every advantage, but I wonder sometimes. That is one question to which I just do not know the answer.

118. Willing One's Body for Research

What do you think about Christians who donate parts of their body for medical research? Or to help someone else?

Dr. Sugden: That is entirely up to you. I think it is great to give your blood to the blood bank. I think it is great to give your eyes, if you feel led to do that. Many of our people are doing it today. They ask me, "Pastor, what do you tell us to do?" I say, "I don't tell you to do anything. Otherwise I have 'Jonestown' on my hands." I don't order peoples' lives, but you are asking me to make a suggestion. Personally, I just want to keep my body intact.

If you are going to donate body parts, you had better check all the rules and regulations of your government. You can make some arrangements ahead of time that will take care of the donation of any part of your body, if this is what you desire. It is entirely up to that individual.

If you donate your eyes, you will still be able to see in your resurrection body. You will have new eyes. When you ask me, personally what I would do, that is something else. I have my own choice about this.

119. Working Women

Please discuss women working outside the home. I feel strongly that the woman's place is in the home. However, our pastor's wife recently started working fulltime. Do you think this is in accordance with the Proverbs 31 description? And what about her example to other ladies in the church?

Mrs. Sugden: Proverbs 31 is quite a description of a mother.

Dr. Sugden: Now, don't get angry with me if I tell you what I think. I, too, think the woman's place is in the home. I know that, financially, it is sometimes an absolute necessity for the mother to work. I realize that, and you yourself know whether you need to or not.

Mrs. Sugden: I think the mother should be in the home when children are small. And then, I don't like this idea of pastors' wives working. I know there are books being written by pastors' wives that say you should "do your own thing." If you have a career, follow it, because you are not hired by the church. I have read these books, but I don't like them. I think a pastor's wife should be with her husband, and they should be a team.

Now, I don't think she should overdo it in the church. I think she should use her spiritual gifts, just like anyone else would. But I feel that the pastor's wife has responsibilities in the home and with her husband. These pastors are not easy to take care of, I tell you. They need a lot of care. I have washed and ironed so many white shirts—a million, I think. You have to keep them dressed well and fed well. I think the place of the pastor's wife is with her husband.

Dr. Sugden: I would underscore that. A husband and wife who have been called to do the work of God should do the work of God. God has a way of taking care of His own, and He never leaves His seed to beg bread.

When we put our energies as a couple into the house of God and the work of God, we become an example to other folk to do the same thing. I like it that way.

120. After Death—Where?

The Bible says that to be absent from the body is to be present with the Lord. Where do we go until the return of our Lord Jesus Christ, at which time we are with Him?

Dr. Sugden: I live with death. That is the field I work in. I received a call from the hospital not long ago. It was the nurse, and she said, "Is this the pastor who specializes in death?"

She was serious. I said, "Yes, I do."

She said, "We need you now. Come, and I will meet you at the desk."

A patient was dying, and somebody needed to be there. Most pastors specialize in death. It is not easy. Someone said to me the other day, after I had lived through three deaths, "How do you endure a day like today?"

Well, you endure because there is going to be a tomorrow, and because some day you are going to be there yourself. Think of this—the very moment I close my eyes here on earth, that moment I open them in heaven! Contrary to the teachings of many cults, the Word of God says that "to be absent from the body is to be at home with the Lord" (see 2 Corinthians 5:8).

The very moment I die, my soul and spirit depart from the body in which I have lived. My body will look very much like it looked before I died, but I will be in heaven. My personality survives; my soul and spirit survive and go to heaven.

I spent years in study and reading on the subject of the intermediate body. I have a strong conviction, borne by the support of many godly scholars, that the moment I die and my soul and spirit leave this body, an intermediate body is given to me. You say, "What makes you think that?"

Look at these verses: "For we know that if our earthly house of this tabernacle were dissolved, we have a building of God, an house not made with hands, eternal in the heavens. For in this body we groan [in this body we groan]. . . ." (2 Cor. 5:1, 2). What do we groan for? We groan "to be clothed upon with our house which is from heaven." And that house which is from heaven is our intermediate body. So I will be in heaven. That is the only way we can know each other in heaven.

How do we get there? My father is there, my mother is there, my brothers are there, my sister is there. How will I know them if they do not have bodies? Who has ever seen a soul?

Souls are invisible. The soul and spirit are the invisible part of me, but when this soul and spirit leave this body, they are clothed with a house which is from heaven. If there should be ten years between now and the return of the Lord Jesus, or a hundred years when the Lord Jesus comes, I am going to come with Him as a believer. You will come with Him as a believer. There will be the voice of the archangel and the trump of God (1 Thess. 4:16, 17), and the dead in Christ will rise first (because they have farther to come). We are there, and we are raised out of the ground. Our bodies are raised, and our resurrected body is merged with our intermediate body at that time. We are caught up with our loved ones, who will be changed, and we will be forever with the Lord Jesus.

121. Food in Heaven

If we have food in heaven, what will it be like?

Dr. Sugden: I think we will have food in heaven. One of the reasons I think so is because when the Lord Jesus stayed for forty days, it says in the margin of your Bible (and the margin of that particular point is correct) in Acts 1:4, "He ate with them."

I don't think you have to have salads for a resurrection body. I don't think you have to have home-made ice cream. But I think we will have food in heaven.

122. Gardens in Heaven

The world began in a garden. I have enjoyed gardening my entire life. Do you think there will be gardens in heaven? Are there any Scripture references?

Dr. Sugden: Yes, it will be full of gardens. Do you know one of the definitions of heaven? It is called "God's Park," because "paradise" means "God's park."

Look at Revelation 22:1, 2: "And he showed me a pure river of water of life, clear as crystal, proceeding out of the throne of God and of the Lamb. In the midst of the street of it and on either side of the river, was there the tree of life, which bare twelve manner of fruits, and yielded her fruit every month . . . "

Everything in Revelation 22 indicates that we are going to have gardens. Heaven and earth will meet in the eternal state, and I think that earth will be renovated, cleansed, and be a part of the eternal state.

There is a book, *The Greater Life and Work of Jesus Christ* by Alexander Patterson. It is about heaven, and the last two chapters of that book deal with the eternal state.

123. Handicapped in Heaven

I am the mother of a handicapped child. Someplace I read a verse that the handicapped will be made whole in heaven. Can you tell me where this is found? What is your interpretation?

Dr. Sugden: In Isaiah 35:1 it says: "The wilderness and the solitary place shall be glad for them; and the desert shall rejoice, and blossom as the rose." This speaks of a future day. There is going to be a day when the wilderness and the solitary place will rejoice.

But now, look at verses 5 and 6: "Then the eyes of the blind shall be opened. Then the ears of the deaf shall be unstopped. Then shall the lame man leap as an hart, and the tongue of the dumb sing..." (Isa. 35:5, 6). All the handicaps will be gone. For many years in our church, we had a section filled with blind children. They came from the School for the Blind. You couldn't miss them as they stood and sang the Doxology. It brought tears to my heart.

People say the "then" has been changed to "now." That's not so! It does not say "*now* the eyes of the blind shall be opened." It says *then.* What a day that will be!

124. Improved Bodies

How will our bodies be improved?

Mrs. Sugden: I have always said, and still think, that our new bodies will be 32 years of age, because that is what the Lord Jesus was, and we will be like Him. Some of us will have to back up a little ways from "39" won't we? I am reminded that even Jesus' new body still had the scars of the crucifixion. Does that mean we will retain marks as a result of sin in this world? No. Are Jesus' scars a reminder to us in heaven of the cost of our salvation? I think so.

Dr. Sugden: By the way, that is an interesting observation. The only One we know of who will be scarred throughout all of eternity will be the Lord Jesus. "But He was wounded for our transgressions, He was bruised for our iniquities: the chastisement of our peace was upon Him; and with His stripes we are healed" (Isa. 53:5).

Through all the ages to come, we will be reminded of His grace in rescuing us by His death on the cross.

125. Intermediate Body

Will our intermediate bodies resemble our personalities? What about age, physical and mental deformities, and sex?

Dr. Sugden: The reason I believe in the intermediate body is this: When Moses and Elijah appeared on the mount of Transfiguration, they had been dead for years—yet they appeared in bodies. There had been no resurrection, but they were people who could be seen. In the Book of Revelation, John saw the saints that had been martyred, so they must have had bodies.

126. Knowledge in Heaven

When our loved ones go to heaven, are they conscious of those left on earth during this day of grace? Will they know if we are suffering?

Dr. Sugden: I do not know any passage in the Word of God that indicates how much knowledge we have in heaven of things that are happening on earth. The evidence seems to be that we know in heaven about the salvation that is being dispensed on earth. I think this is true. It says that "there is joy in the presence of the angels of God" (Luke 15:10). It does not say there is joy among the angels. We always misread that verse and say there is joy among the angels. No, there is joy "in the presence of the angels."

Now the only folk who are in the presence of the angels, other than God the Father and God the Son, are the saints in heaven. So I gather that in heaven there is some way that God communicates, to those who are there, how the work is going on earth.

There are those who teach from Hebrews 12:1, 2 that those in heaven are observing us on earth. Hebrews 12 is a picture of an athletic contest. It is a picture of a stadium filled with people. The question is, Are they observing us, or are we observing them?

I think we are observing them. They have run the race. They

have taken their places in the stands, and we are to run the race as they ran it. We are to run it with faithfulness. That passage, in my judgment, does not teach that folk in the stands are watching us on earth.

Now, do the folk in the stands know something about what is happening on earth? I think two or three passages indicate something about this.

First, there is the account of the Lord Jesus and the Transfiguration. It is found in Matthew 17, Mark 9, and Luke 9. Moses and Elijah appeared with the Lord Jesus on the mountain of Transfiguration. Peter and James and John were there. That was a wonderful scene. Imagine climbing that mountain, and there heaven comes down! The residents of heaven are there.

Do you know what they want to talk about? They are not talking about the weather, or the financial condition of Israel. They are talking with the men on earth about the events that were going to happen on earth. They said, "How are plans coming for the cross?" They talked about the death Jesus would die on the cross. So it is evident that they knew something about what was going to transpire on that lonely hill outside the city wall.

There is another occasion, in the Book of Revelation (Rev. 6:10), where the martyrs who are in heaven look down on earth. They are crying out about the condition of things on earth, and saying, "How long will it be before God moves and takes over this crowd on earth?" So they knew what was happening.

Then remember the parables in Luke 15? There are the parables of the sheep, of the coin, and of the son. In the parable of the sheep, it is the lost lamb. When it is found, there is joy in the presence of the angels of God over one sinner who turns to Christ. So it is evident that when something happens redemptively here on earth, something happens in heaven.

I think we dare, from these three pictures given to us in the New Testament, say that the saints in heaven are aware of the redemptive movements of God on earth. I personally believe that they are aware in heaven of all the redemptive acts on earth, and of the progress of the kingdom of our Lord and His Christ upon this earth.

That makes heaven a great place. How are things going today? Just think, the newspapers of heaven had headlines about what happened in church last night!

127. New Body

If our bodies in the grave return to dust, and we're going to receive new bodies, why should the old body be resurrected?

Dr. Sugden: The resurrection of the body is to me one of the great and precious truths of the Word of God. The Bible says: "Beloved, now are we sons of God, and it doth not yet appear what we shall be: but we know that, when He shall appear, we shall be like Him . . ." (1 John 3:2).

If we believe this, then we have a pattern of the resurrection body. Jesus died. He didn't swoon or faint. The coolness of the grave did not revive Him, like some people say. He died! The gospel is that Christ died for our sins according to the Scriptures. He was buried, and He arose the third day. Decomposition had begun in his body. Now when the Lord Jesus arose, did He have the body in which He died?

The body in which He arose had no physical limitations. It had the nail prints. The scars were in His side. When they looked on Him, they saw Him as He was when he walked on earth. There is a great mystery about this.

Philippians 3 is a significant passage of one of the basic truths for which we as evangelical believers stand: that Jesus Christ died, that He rose again, and that we will share in that resurrection. I am confident of that. "For our citizenship is in heaven . . ." (Phil. 3:20).

We are citizens of two worlds—visible and invisible. In the visible we are citizens of Canada or the United States, or wherever; but we are also citizens of heaven, ". . . from whence also we look for the Savior, the Lord Jesus Christ" (Phil. 3:20).

Now note what He is going to do: "Who shall change our vile body . . ." (Phil. 3:21). If you have a margin in your Bible, it says, "who shall change our body of humiliation." Our body is not vile in the sense of things being vile. Our body was humiliated in the fall. It is not like it was when it came from the hand of God. We have sickness in our bodies; we have infirmities in our bodies. Our bodies have all the marks of a catastrophe.

But now note that He is going to ". . . change our vile body [our body of humiliation] that it may be fashioned like unto His glorious body" (Phil. 3:21). So again Paul underscored what John wrote in 1 John 3:1, 2, that we will be like Christ. Our bodies will be like His glorious body.

If we stopped here, you'd say, "Well, that's almost enough,

Pastor. I don't need any more. It is enough. I would believe that there is going to be a resurrection of the body, if I found it in only this one place."

I cannot explain the resurrection. I do know that it is going to happen, and that it involves our body, the body that it is sown in the ground. "But some man will say, How are the dead raised up? and with what body do they come? Thou fool, that which thou soweth is not quickened, except it die" (1 Cor. 15:35, 36).

That is true! Everything around us comes out of death. You drop a seed in the soil. How do you get something from that seed? It dies. After we planted potatoes, my father would find a place where there were no potatoes growing. He could reach down with his big hand and scoop out the dirt and find a potato that had never died. It was just like it was when it was planted. For all the plants that had potatoes, the seed had died. This is a mystery. The seed produces a potato just like the potato it came from, yet it is a different potato, isn't it?

"...that which thou sowest is not quickened, except it die; and that which thou soweth, thou soweth not that body that shall be, but bare grain, it may chance of wheat, or of some other grain: but God giveth it a body as it hath pleased Him..." (1 Cor. 15:36-38).

So God gives it a body as it pleases Him, and to every seed his own body. So I won't come with someone else's body. It says: "...to every seed his own body" (1 Cor. 15:38).

Then Paul goes on to describe that there is one kind of flesh of men, another flesh of beasts, another of fishes, and another of birds. And then verse 42: "So also is the resurrection of the dead." Think of this: "So also is the resurrection of the dead."

"It is sown in corruption; it is raised in incorruption. It is sown in dishonor; it is raised in glory; it is sown in weakness; it is raised in power. It is sown a natural body; it is raised a spiritual body. There is a natural body, and there is a spiritual body. And so it is written, The first man Adam was made a living soul; the last Adam was made a quickening spirit. Howbeit that was not first which is spiritual, but that which is natural; and afterward that which is spiritual" (1 Cor. 15:42-46).

Put a little note there. This is a divine principle all the way through the Word of God. You always have the natural person first and the spiritual afterward. That is the divine order: natural man, spiritual man. Wherever you have twins, or have people linked together in the Bible, the first one is the natural, and the second one is the spiritual. Remember that. It is the way God operates.

> "The first man is of the earth, earthy; the second man is the Lord from heaven: As is the earthy, such are they also that are earthy: and as is the heavenly, such are they also that are heavenly. And as we have borne the image of the earth [Adam], we shall also bear the image of the heavenly " (1 Cor. 15:47-49).

Now verse 51: "Behold, I show you a mystery; We shall not all sleep, but we shall all be changed." No partial rapture! If there were ever a church that could have had a partial rapture, it would have been the Corinthian church, because they were carnal and worldly folks. God could have said, "I'm going to leave the carnal and the worldly ones here." But He said, "We shall not all sleep, but we shall all be changed, in a moment, in the twinkling of an eye" (1 Cor. 15:51, 52). That word, "twink" is a great word. A twink is quicker than a wink. Did you know that? I can see you wink, but I can't see you twink. You'll be changed like that—in the twinkling of an eye.

This is not easy to grasp. But as certain as you have been in this body, and this body is sown in the earth, there is going to be a resurrection of your body. We will know each other in heaven. We will remember in heaven. We will have all the time we need to go back over all the good experiences. And we'll be together for all of eternity.

128. Number of Occupants in Heaven

Will there be more souls in heaven or in hell?

Dr. Sugden: All the theologians know Benjamin Breckenridge Warfield. He said there will be more in heaven than in hell. I think that Warfield went back in his thought process and said, "Think of the millions of children who have died before the age of accountability who all go to heaven."

As Wesley once said (and only Wesley could say this): "There will be three surprises in heaven. You'll be surprised when you look for some people and they are not there. You'll be surprised when you meet somebody there you didn't expect. And then you'll be surprised that you are there." That's the way Wesley thought.

129. Out-of-body Experiences

Concerning the close relationship between the natural and spiritual worlds, what do you think about people who have had out-of-body experiences when seriously ill or injured? When they recover they tell of light, a tunnel, or stairs. They even have the feeling that they are outside their bodies looking down and watching the doctors work on them.

Dr. Sugden: Many books have been published on this. I don't know why I do such stupid things, but I buy them and read them. I have great doubts about many of these experiences.

I think some of the books written by doctors are probably authoritative and can be documented. But I do not believe that we leave our bodies and circle around the operating room, or look in and see the doctor sewing us up while we are outside.

We can do great things in writing, but the fact is that the Word of God says that the body without the spirit is dead. That is finality. When your spirit leaves your body, your body is dead. Can all these things happen, and the person is not dead? The body without the spirit is dead.

Mrs. Sugden: Remember, drugs will give you hallucinations.

Dr. Sugden: And some wild ones too. We have wild hallucinations on our streets and in our hospitals.

130. Purgatory

I have a sister-in-law who feels bad because her mother is in purgatory. I told her we do not believe in purgatory, but that the Bible says, "Absent from the body is to be present with the Lord" for believers.

Mrs. Sugden: We don't believe there is such a thing as purgatory.

Dr. Sugden: It is hard to discover when purgatory became a doctrine in the Roman Catholic church, but it was well along in the life of the church. The reason we do not believe in purgatory is because it is not taught in the Word of God. The closest word to it is in Hebrews 1, where it says of Christ that "when He had by himself purged our sins, sat down at the right hand of the Majesty on high" (Hebrews 1:3). That is the nearest thing to purgatory in the New Testament—and this is not purgatory!

Purgatory is a doctrine of the church that cannot be substantiated by the Holy Scripture.

131. Remembrance in Heaven

Isaiah 65:17 says that God will create a new heaven and a new earth, and the former shall not be remembered nor come into mind. Does this mean that Christians will not be able to remember the griefs and hurts they experienced on earth? Will they forget those loved ones not in heaven with them?

Dr. Sugden: The verse reads: "For, behold, I create new heavens and a new earth: and the former shall not be remembered, nor come into mind" (Isa. 65:17). I'm sure that this is true, because heaven is not a place where we will agonize about the sorrows and disappointments that happened in this life.

Heaven is going to be occupation with God, with Christ, and with all the glories and wonders of God's creation. I gather that we will be occupied with the things God has planned for us.

This is not out of context, but some people quote, "Eye hath not seen, nor ear heard, neither have entered into the heart of man, the things which God hath prepared for them that love Him" (1 Cor. 2:9).

I take that out of context by saying that this truth can be applied to all of God's tomorrows for us. We have not the faintest concept of all that is going to happen. For a moment, at this Bible conference, we are in conversation with people and we move about the grounds. The pressures and the sorrows we had yesterday are almost forgotten in the light of the joys we have today.

If this is true in the very limited sphere I speak of now, what must it be like to be in heaven and have no more sorrows and turmoils of life? It is going to be a great place.

132. Tears in Heaven

Will there be tears in heaven?

Dr. Sugden: What I think will cause the tears that the Lord will wipe away is when we appear before the judgment seat of Christ. Some will receive no rewards. You have to be careful about that.

One thing you have to remember about the judgment seat of Christ is that it is not a place where God is whipping people. I used to think that. I heard a man preach on that once, and that is the way it was. God would expose everybody who had been lazy, mean, or whatever. I don't think so.

Paul wrote of the judgment seat of Christ, 1 Corinthians 4:5, and says, ". . . Then shall every man have praise of God." The first time I saw that verse, I said, "There must be a mistake." Paul was talking about Christians. When a Christian stands before the Lord at the judgment seat (not the Great White

Throne, for we will never meet there to be judged for our sins),
". . . then shall every man have praise of God."

I think the praise comes because we accepted Jesus Christ. He
will praise us for that. Beyond that come the rewards.

133. Telling Children About Heaven

*How would you answer an 8-year-old child who asks, "How
did Jesus take Grandpa from here to heaven?" I explained as
well as I could about the body, soul and spirit, and I think she
understood a little.*

Dr. Sugden: I would probably answer just the way you did.
We can illustrate with children to help them understand. I
don't think God sends 727's to get us. But I do believe that
heaven is very real to children.

Don't be afraid to talk to children about these things. I think
of the kids on the front seats of our church. Imagine three little
guys sitting on the front seat. This is in church, and I said,
"How are you fellows tonight?"

"Oh," they said, "are we ever beat."

I thought, At ten years old? What'll they do when they get to
be sixty, if they're beat at ten?

But here is this chubby little guy. He always sat right in front
of me. His home was pretty rough at times. One day his mother
called me. She said, "Oh, Pastor, this must have been a great
morning at church. Johnny came home and said that you talked
about heaven this morning. He told me he would like to go
there today."

Children are very serious about death, and we explain it to
them. If you take them to funerals, they see bodies. You have to
explain that this is Grandpa or auntie or your uncle. You have
to explain that only the body is in the casket. They ask you,
"Where are they?" They have gone. They have taken the en-
gine out of the chassis. They have taken the soul and the spirit
out of the body. Who has done that?

Then you tell them that God loves them and cares for them.
They are His children, and He has taken them to heaven. Isn't it
interesting that when you have pictures of this, you have angels
who do it. He sent the angel to take the man at the gate who had
died. So angels are God's ministering servants. The man in
Luke 16 was taken into heaven by the angels.

It's a great thing to tell a child, "Well, an angel came and took Grandpa. God liked Grandpa so much He wanted him in heaven. So He sent the angel.''

When I have funerals, I try to leave this wonderful thought about death: How wonderful to step out of a visible world into the invisible world of God and to be in heaven.

So we teach children about death when they are young, and they never forget it.

134. What Happens to the Soul?

Do you believe that when a Christian dies, the soul stays with the body until Christ comes? Please quote Scripture to support your answer.

Dr. Sugden: Let me make a statement and then prove the statement. We are a tripartite being. We have a body, soul, and spirit. The soul and spirit are the motor of your life to keep you alive.

In James 2:26 we read that ''the body without the spirit is dead.'' Amazing statement! The moment I die, the spirit leaves my body. At that very moment I enter into the presence of God.

Here are two verses. ''For me to live is Christ, and to die is gain'' (Phil. 1:21). Then verse 23: ''For I am in a straight betwixt two, having a desire to depart, and to be with Christ . . .'' He said, ''I have a desire to die.'' Why? The word ''depart'' is ''die.'' It is this word ''exodus,'' and when I die I will be with Christ—which is far better. It is not better to be taken out and put into the ground, but it is better when you go to be with Christ. And you go to be with Him immediately.

Where is Christ? He is in heaven. How do we know that He is in heaven? In the first chapter of Acts we read that while the apostles looked up into heaven, Jesus was taken up from them into heaven. And Paul says that when I die, I will go to be with Christ. He is in heaven. In 2 Corinthians 5 we read these amazing words: ''For we know that if our earthly house of this tabernacle were dissolved . . .'' (2 Cor. 5:1).

Paul said we know something about death. We don't have to buy books that only multiply ignorance. We can read the Word of God, which talks about death. Note what he says: ''Therefore, we are always confident, knowing that, whilst we are at home in our body'' [while we are here in our body we are not with the Lord] ''we are absent from the Lord. (For we walk by faith, not by sight:) We are confident, I say, and willing rather

to be absent from the body, and to be present with the Lord"
(2 Cor. 5:6-8).

Just think—absent from the body, present with the Lord!
Absent here, present there.

Now you ask, "How does all this get started that the soul
stays with the body? This is the teaching of our Adventist
friends. Many other groups also say that people die and
are buried.

They go back and accumulate Old Testament texts. May I
remind you that when you accumulate Old Testament texts on
the subject of death, you only multiply your problem. When
you read Paul's letter to Timothy this is what Paul said to
Timothy about Jesus Christ: He ". . .brought life and immor-
tality to light through the gospel" (2 Tim. 1:10).

They didn't have this light in the Old Testament. We have it
now. We do not have proof texts on heaven from the Old
Testament, but we do from the New. And it says that to be
absent from the body is to be home with the Lord. I'm glad
that on the day I close my eyes here, I will go immediately
to heaven.

135. When Do We Enter Heaven?

*After we die, when do we go to heaven? Jesus told the thief on
the cross, "This day you will be with Me in heaven." But
Scripture tells us that when Jesus comes again, the dead in
Christ will rise first.*

Dr. Sugden: I will be in heaven the very moment I die. The
moment the thief on the cross died, he went directly to heaven.

Spurgeon was great on this topic. He had everybody in
heaven looking out over us saying, "Look who's coming."
They look out, and there is Jesus, and He is coming into heaven.
And the dying thief enters heaven.

You go to heaven the very moment you die, because you are a
tripartite being. You have a body, soul, and spirit. Two parts of
you never die. They go immediately to heaven. Your body goes
to the grave. When the Lord Jesus comes again, He brings your
soul and spirit. They are united with your resurrected body.

9
THE HOLY SPIRIT

136. The Holy Spirit in the Old Testament

Did the believers in the Old Testament have the indwelling of the Holy Spirit when they accepted God, since Jesus was not born until the New Testament?

Mrs. Sugden: You will find in the Old Testament that the Holy Spirit came upon people, but He departed. He came at different times for different purposes. When the Lord Jesus was here, He promised the disciples: "And I will pray the Father, and He shall give you another Comforter, that He may *abide* with you forever" (John 14:16).

FOREVER: Did you notice that? "Even the Spirit of truth; whom the world cannot receive, because it seeth Him not, neither knoweth Him: but ye know Him; for He dwelleth with you, and shall be in you" (John 14:17).

Then in John 16:7, "Nevertheless, I tell you the truth; It is expedient for you that I go away: for if I go not away, the Comforter will not come unto you; but if I depart, I will send Him unto you."

When we receive Christ, the Holy Spirit comes to dwell *in us* *forever.* He did not in the Old Testament. It began the day of Pentecost.

Dr. Sugden: Isn't it amazing and thrilling to think about this passage? Jesus said, "I'm going to go to the Father, and when I arrive at the Father's house, I'm going to pray the Father, and He will send the Holy Spirit."

I had an old friend, and every morning when we came to the preacher's meetings, he would say, "Well, today we'll pray for the Spirit to come."

I told him that bothered me, because he was 1900 years too late. We don't have to pray for the Spirit of God. When the Lord Jesus arrived in heaven, He prayed—and think of what happened on the day of Pentecost! Peter said in Acts 2:33, "[He] being by the right hand of God exalted, . . . hath shed forth this, which ye now see and hear."

Peter said that the Holy Spirit is coming here today. His

baptizing us into one body is an evidence that Christ has arrived in heaven. He has been there ever since. He is there now as our Great High Priest. And our Great High Priest is there to help us in our hour of need. When we need strength, He gives us strength. So He is there, the Lord Jesus, at the right hand of the Father. He prays for us.

137. The Holy Spirit at Pentecost

In Acts 1:8 we read, "Ye shall receive power, after that the Holy Ghost is come upon you." What is your interpretation of this verse?

Dr. Sugden: If you go through the gospels and the Book of Acts, once in each book a pronouncement is made. John the Baptist made the pronouncement. He said, "He shall baptize you in the Holy Ghost" (John 1:33; Matthew 3:11; Mark 1:8; Luke 3:16). In Acts 1, after the Lord Jesus was raised from the dead, it is mentioned that He will baptize you with the Holy Spirit not many days hence."

So it pinpoints a day. On the day of Pentecost the Holy Spirit came. The disciples had believed on the Lord Jesus, and now the Holy Spirit came on the day of Pentecost to indwell them. This meant that they would have God's power in their lives. He came to baptize them into the body of Christ.

138. Indwelling of the Holy Spirit

Acts 11:17 says, "Forasmuch then as God gave them the like gift as He did unto us, who believed on the Lord Jesus Christ; what was I, that I could withstand God?" Does this mean that Peter and the other apostles didn't believe in Jesus until the day of Pentecost, when they were baptized by the Holy Spirit?

Dr. Sugden: No. They believed in Him and they followed Him. But you see, the day of Pentecost was a special day in the economy of God. It was a day that will never be repeated.

When I have well-meaning friends who have set aside 2 days to pray for a Pentecost, they are 1900 years too late and they are 8,000 miles away from the spot where that happened on the day of Pentecost.

Pentecost is not repeated. Pentecost was a day in the plan and program of God, as much a day as the cross. The cross is never repeated. The resurrection is never repeated. The *blessing* of the cross repeated? Yes! The *blessings* of the resurrection repeated? Yes! And the *blessings* of Pentecost are repeated, but never the *day*. It happened once in history. It was the day that the Holy Spirit of God came, to first of all baptize the believers into one body, and then to indwell them. They had not been indwelt until that day.

When Peter talked about the gift, it is the gift of the Holy Spirit of God that came on that day. The disciples were not filled with the Spirit or indwelt with the Spirit before Pentecost.

The were indwelt, filled, in Acts 2. It was that day, the day of Pentecost, when they were filled. They followed Him, and they believed in Him, but on *that* day they were baptized into the body, and on *that* day they were filled with the Holy Spirit of God.

The moment you believed in Jesus Christ as your Savior, at *that* moment you were baptized by the Holy Spirit into the body of Christ (1 Cor. 12:13). That is the only way you get into the body of Christ. Never once are we ever encouraged to have the baptism of the Holy Spirit. There isn't one word in the New Testament that encourages anyone to be baptized by the Spirit. Why? Because it happens the moment you believe.

We are encouraged to be filled, but we are never encouraged to be baptized. That is something we don't have anything to do with. It is not of human hands. The Lord Jesus baptizes us with the Holy Spirit when we believe, and then we are to be filled. So Peter said exactly what we say. He was referring to the Gentiles. You see, there were two groups: Jews and Gentiles. Peter was saying the Gentiles had the baptism of the Holy Spirit the same as the Jews.

You can pray for the baptism of the Holy Spirit all night long, and you will never get it. You already have it, if you believe.

139. Broken Body

In the King James Version of 1 Corinthians 11:24 we read that Jesus said, ". . . This is My body, which is broken for you . . ." How come that not once do we read the word "broken" in this context in the gospels?

Dr. Sugden: Isn't it strange that all my life this has never bothered me? I have quoted that passage in 1 Corinthians many times. Why has it never bothered me? Because I think everyone understands that Jesus was speaking about the life that was forfeited and given. It was in the breaking of His body that His life was given, and that of course, is the interpretation.

Christ's life was given; His blood and body. He gave His blood; He gave His body. His blood was shed. His body was broken. And it is in the shedding of His blood and the brokenness of His body that we have eternal life. There is no other way.

Isaiah 53:5 says, "He was wounded for our transgressions; He was bruised for our iniquities . . ." Someone could say, "Well, the lamb for sacrifice in the Old Testament was not to have any broken bones. That is why the Lord's legs were not broken at the cross, like the other men's were. He fulfilled exactly the Scriptures."

The passage is not talking about brokenness in the sense of breaking something. It is in the sense of life being given.

140. Christ's Sinless Perfection

Could Jesus have sinned when tempted by Satan, or at any other time? Did he have the capability to disobey His Father? If not, what was the main purpose of His testing?

Dr. Sugden: Jesus was tested, not to see if He would sin, but to prove that He couldn't sin. I have friends who disagree with me. But I believe the Word of God teaches the impeccability of Jesus Christ. If He could have sinned on earth, He could sin now, because He is the "same yesterday, and today and forever." Although Christ did have a body, He was God while He was in that body. He was God with us, so I think the testing was there to prove He could not sin.

The nicest thing I ever read about this was in some little messages put out in a tract, when this issue was a battleground. For ages people have battled about the peccability of Christ (His ability to sin) and the impeccability of Christ (that He won't sin).

Dr. I. M. Haldeman, who was then pastor of the First Baptist Church in New York City, had a cottage out in the mountains. The New York Central, one of the great railroads, put a huge bridge across one of the great chasms between the mountains. With all of their genius of structure and steel they raised this bridge and finally completed it. The day came when it would be tested.

He said he saw the engineers drive locomotive engines each with a loaded freight car behind it, one from each direction, meet and pass in the middle on double tracks. Each engineer pulled the throttle and the old wheels began to spin. Dr. Haldeman said, "I looked out and I learned that they were *not* doing this to prove the bridge would break. They did it to prove that the bridge would *not* break."

Then he said that when our Lord was tested, He was tested in order to prove He would not and could not fail. Everyone who later rode on those railroads across that long span looked out and knew it couldn't break. It had been tested. So with Christ.

141. Deity of Christ

In John 10:34-36 it seems Jesus is disclaiming His deity by equalling Himself with the Old Testament judges (Psalm 82:6), who were called gods. Why did Jesus use such an argument? Didn't the Jews have the right to stone Jesus for blasphemy, according to their beliefs after Jesus' statement in John 10:30?

Dr. Sugden: They picked up stones because Jesus had said, "I and My Father are one." Then the Jews took up stones to stone Him. They said, "Here's a man who says He is God."

Now, what was Jesus' response to this? "Jesus answered them, Many good works have I shewed you from My Father; for which of those works do you stone me?" (John 10:32).

What are you stoning Me for? Are you stoning Me because I multiplied the loaves and fishes? No one else had ever done that. Are you stoning Me because I quieted the storm and the sea? Are you stoning Me because I lifted the eyes of the blind and opened them? Are you stoning Me for that? He said, "Which one of the good works are you stoning Me for?"

And, of course, there was a hush—because no one had ever done what He had done. Now when they were quiet, "the Jews answered Him saying, For a good work we stone Thee not, but for blasphemy; and because that Thou, being a man, makest Thyself God" (John 10:33).

They said, "We are not stoning you because you have been so good. We're stoning you because you blaspheme in saying you're God."

Now listen to Jesus' answer: "Jesus answered them, Is it not written [and it was in the 82nd Psalm] in your law, I said, Ye are gods?" (John 10:34). Jesus is referring to men. God has said that they were gods; that is, they were different from all the rest of God's creation. They were a special creation.

Now, this is His argument: "If He called them gods, to whom the word of God came [He said the Word of God came to them], and the Scriptures cannot be broken; [He said that it stands] say ye of Him, whom the Father [He said that if it stands in the Old Testament that they are gods, how much more should you reverence Me because the Father] hath sanctified, and sent into the world" (John 10:35, 36).

He never sanctified and sent them, but He has sent Christ. And He said, "If I do not the works of My Father, believe Me not" (John 10:37).

Jesus was not stooping down. He was just saying once again to them that He is the One that God has sent and that God has sanctified. Then He said: "But if I do not the works of My Father, believe Me not. But if I do, though you believe not Me, believe the works; that ye may know, and believe that the Father is in Me, and I in Him" (John 10:37-38). Jesus affirmed His deity.

142. Forsaken by God

Why did God have to turn away from Jesus on the cross because of the sin put on Him? He talked face to face with Satan concerning Job?

Dr. Sugden: On that cross more than 1900 years ago, God placed on His Son our sin—all of it. The totality of sin was placed on the Lord Jesus. "Thou [God] art of purer eyes than to behold evil'' we read in Habakkuk 1:13. Therefore, the Father turned His face momentarily from His Son.

It is an entirely different situation with Satan. Satan is the adversary. Satan brought about sin. He was never a sin-bearer. Satan was the one who used sin to destroy, and so God had a right to confront him, to talk face to face with him.

143. Redemptive Work

How extensive is the finished work of Christ?

Dr. Sugden: For how many people did Christ die? First, look at this verse: ''The next day John seeth Jesus coming unto Him, and sayeth, 'Behold the Lamb of God, which taken away the sin of the world'.''

Now look at John 3:17, ''For God sent not His Son into the world to condemn the world; but that the world through Him might be saved.''

And John 4:42, ''And said unto the woman, 'Now we believe, not because of thy saying: for we have heard Him ourselves, and know that this is indeed the Christ, the Savior of the WORLD'.''

John 6:33, ''For the bread of God is He which cometh down from heaven, and giveth life unto the WORLD.''

John 6:51, ''I am the living bread which came down from heaven: if any man eat of this bread, he shall live forever: and the bread that I will give is My flesh, which I will give for the life of the WORLD.''

John 12:47, ''And if any man hear My words, and believe not, I judge him not: for I came not to judge the world, but to save the WORLD.''

These verses are of vital importance when you think about how wide is the reach of Christ's redemptive work. A man by the name of Kittle has written ten volumes of word studies. In one of these he deals with the word ''world.'' It has to do with the world where I live, and it has to do with the world of man.

Romans 3:21, 22, ''But now the righteousness of God without the law is manifested, being witnessed by the law and the prophets; Even the righteousness of God which is by faith of Jesus Christ UNTO ALL and upon all them that believe: for there is no difference.''

Now look at Romans 11:32, ''For God hath concluded them all in unbelief.'' Who has He concluded in unbelief? All the

Jews, all the Gentiles, all men. He has concluded them in unbelief "that He might have mercy upon *ALL*."

144. Resurrection Power

What does it mean "to know Him and the power of His resurrection" in Philippians 3:10?

Dr. Sugden: I think it means exactly what it says. When Paul wrote this in Philippians 3, he was talking about the power that raised Jesus Christ from the dead. He is saying to me today that the same power indwells me as a Christian as that which raised Jesus Christ from the dead.

If you want to see something of the mightiness of the power of God, come and see an empty tomb. Understand there is a risen Christ. And then understand that the same power that raised Christ from the dead lives in you. He is in you—that same power!

145. Son of Man

Do you think there is any significance to the fact that Jesus in the New Testament is called Son of Man so many more times than Son of God?

Dr. Sugden: There is a rule of hermeneutics, which is the art of biblical interpretation, that an author reveals his point of view in his stress upon words and events and ideas.

Now what does that say? That was one of the first great rules of biblical interpretation that I learned from one of the greatest English Bible teachers that ever lived, Howard Tilman Kuist. That was his great word—that an author in the Word of God, who is moved by the Spirit of God, reveals his point of view by his stress upon words. Therefore, when you read the Book of Hebrews, you find out that the word "better" is used over and over again. You understand that the writer is talking about something that is better than anything has been before. It just pops out at you.

Compare how often the phrase "Son of God" is used and the number of times "Son of Man" is used. I believe it was because people have more difficulty in accepting the fact that Jesus Christ was the Son of God as He walked as a Man, than they do in accepting Him as the Son of Man.

It is hard to believe that God, the eternal God, became a baby.

Paul, in Colossians, says that "by Him [the Lord Jesus] were all things created that are in heaven and that are on earth."

Here is the mighty Creator of the universe . . . and He is a baby. The One who created all things now becomes dependent. He was clutched to His mother's breast. He was a little boy. He was a teenager. Did you ever think that Jesus was a teenager? That he was a young man? He grew to maturity. He was God.

You say, "Oh, it can't be. It baffles my imagination. It baffles my mind."

But for that very reason Jesus said He was the Son of Man. He said it so we will understand. I believe it, because I have walked with Him for fifty-nine years, and in this He is identified with me. He is identified with the teenager. He was a junior-higher once. His mother used to take Him by the hand and lead Him to the synagogue. So He was identified with us.

146. Tell No Man

In some cases Jesus said, "Return to thine own house and shew how great things God hath done unto thee" (Luke 8:39). Yet in other cases He said, "Tell no man" (Luke 8:56). Why?

Dr. Sugden: Because our Lord was running a life that was on the schedule of heaven, He was moving in the will of God. There would come a time when He would be able to make Himself known, but for this particular time and in that particular situation He was not to tell it.

There would come a time when His identity would be declared openly. Different situations arose, and each situation was handled differently. It was because of the time element, and the element of scheduling, that He did or did not want His identity known.

147. Touch Not

When Jesus appeared to Mary after the resurrection, He said to her, "Touch me not; for I am not yet ascended to my Father" (John 20:17). But in John 20:27, Jesus told Thomas to "reach hither thy hand, and thrust it into My side." Why did Jesus tell Mary not to touch Him, and yet invite Thomas to put his hand in His side?

Dr. Sugden: It doesn't have anything to do with women's liberation, I assure you. I believe that the answer is not a surface answer, but is bound up with the Old Testament priesthood.

On the day of atonement, when the high priest laid aside his robes of glory, he put on his linen robes and made the atonement that was essential for Israel. No one was to touch him until his work has been completed—no one! But after the work was completed, he could be touched.

Now our Lord has died and He has just risen when He spoke to Mary. I believe that the completion of His work was to enter heaven. I think He entered heaven, between then and the time when He met with the disciples, and presented Himself to the Father as the High Priest who had performed all the functions to remove sins. Now He was touchable!

That seems to me to be a most wonderful truth. Our Lord said, "Don't touch Me now; handle Me not," and then He came back and said, "Now you can touch me."

148. Was Jesus in Hell?

Did Jesus really descend into hell after he died?

Dr. Sugden: When the Lord Jesus was on the cross He said to the dying thief, "Today shalt thou be with Me in Paradise". (Luke 23:43). Luke 23:46 says, "And when Jesus had cried with a loud voice, He said, Father, into thy hand I commend My spirit." The question then is where did Jesus go and why?

He dismissed His spirit to the Father. His body was taken down at sundown and laid in the sepulcher. His soul descended to Sheol, the same place Abel and all the saints of the Old Testament down to John the Baptist had gone, awaiting the coming of the Redeemer to finish their redemption.

The Old Testament saints were prisoners of hope in the Paradise section of Sheol (Hebrew name or Hades in Greek or Hell in English).

Their hope was well expressed in Psalm 16:10, "for thou wilt not let my soul in Sheol."

When the full price of their redemption was paid by Christ, He went to Sheol to minister to these spirits in prison and to release them. Many believe this, for in 1 Peter 3:19, it says, "He went and preached to the spirits in prison."

When Christ arose, He took all those Old Testament saints out of Sheol, "led captivity captive" (Psalm 68:18; Eph. 4:8). That is, He took the saints up and set up a Paradise above. Since the resurrection of Christ, all believers when they die go up.

Remember the Apostle Paul, stoned and left for dead at Lystra said, "I was caught up into the third heaven into Paradise" (Acts 14:19) (2 Cor 12:2, 4).

When we were children and I went to the little Methodist Church in our town, we repeated the Apostles' Creed. We always said that Jesus descended into hell and the third day He arose from the dead and ascended into heaven.

149. What Day Was Christ Crucified?

Some say Christ spent 3 days and 3 nights in the earth. How then do we recognize Friday as the crucifixion day?

Dr. Sugden: We will get our answer to that from the Word of God: "Jesus began to show His disciples how He must go to Jerusalem, suffer many things of the chief priests and scribes, and be killed and be raised again the third day" (Matt. 20:19).

In Luke's account, we have these events (Luke 23:54-56). "And that day was the day of preparation and the Sabbath drew near . . . beheld the sepulcher, and how His body was laid. And they returned, prepared spices and ointments, and rested on the Sabbath day." In Luke 24:1, 2, we read, "Now upon the first day of the week, very early in the morning, they came to the sepulcher, bringing the spices they had prepared . . . and they found the stone rolled away."

In Acts 10:40, notice "Him God raised up the third day and showed Him openly, not to all people but to witnesses . . . even to us."

And again in 1 Corinthians 15:4, Paul indicates the faith of the early Christians. "And that He was buried and that He arose again the third day, according to the Scriptures."

11
MARRIAGE AND DIVORCE

150. Annulment

Why is annulment acceptable and not divorce?

Dr. Sugden: I fear that the position of the Roman Catholic church has kept Protestants from honestly surveying the problem of divorce and remarriage. One day a man told me that his church was far superior, because they didn't have divorce in their church.

But I have news. While they may not get a divorce, there are twenty-two reasons why they can get an annulment. For instance, if a woman can prove that her husband did not expect to have children when he married her, she can get an annulment.

We have to read and study the Word of God, and find in it there is forgiveness for divorce. Divorce is not the unpardonable sin. The Lord does forgive, and He does restore.

Someone says, "Pastor, you make it too easy, don't you?"

"No, I don't." Every divorce that comes into our house of God leaves me with a broken heart. It hurts me. I don't want to see any home broken.

151. Attending a Catholic Wedding

Should a born-again Christian attend a niece's wedding in a Roman Catholic church? If you attend, does it mean that you condone it?

Dr. Sugden: You would not believe how many times this has come up in our church. I have had families almost separated because of conflict over this type of question.

Let me tell you what happened in a similar case. A father came in to see me about his own daughter. He said, "I refuse to go to her wedding in that Catholic Church."

I said, "I think you are making a mistake."

I have no traffic with Roman Catholics and their theology and what they believe. But I said to him, "Your family is at stake, you home is at stake, and your wife is at stake. Sometime along the way, your daughter will need you. You are throwing blocks in the way. Now stick all your pride in your pocket, and all your theological teaching (for a while) in your pocket, and go down there and be a Christian.''

152. Divorce and Remarriage

How do you handle the problem of divorce and remarriage for Christians?

Dr. Sugden: God put His ideal in the book of Genesis when He said: ''Therefore shall a man leave his father and his mother, and shall cleave unto his wife: and they shall be one flesh'' (Gen. 2:24).

When He was here on earth, Jesus said that the original intention of God would be monogamy—one man and one woman. But because of the hardness of men's hearts, God made some exceptions. I have studied this for over forty years. You don't give an answer off the top of your head and say, ''Oh, I guess it's like this.'' God is not ever giving His approval and saying, ''Yes, this is fine.'' But He is saying that because of the perverseness of man, He allows certain things.

In Matthew 19, the Lord was talking to Jewish people, a man or woman who committed adultery. In that context and framework, they would be a part of God's family. Jesus said that if the husband leaves, commits adultery, or if the woman commits adultery, the marriage tie is broken.

I have a friend who says that the moment that happens, the marriage tie is broken and severed. Now, it doesn't mean that a husband has to leave or a wife has to leave, but the marriage tie is severed. Sin has severed it. In that severance, according to Matthew, the innocent party has a right to secure divorce.

We also have reference to this in 1 Corinthians 7. We live in an hour when we just can't poke our heads in the sand and say, ''I want to ignore it.'' We have to deal with people's needs. The ideal is no divorce, no remarriage. But what are you going to do when you live in a situation like this? I believe that it is because God knew a situation like this would come that He allowed Matthew 19 to be where it is, and 1 Corinthians 7 to be where it is.

The sections in the gospel almost seem like parallel passages. Jesus is talking to the scribes and Pharisees. They know all about the Jewish law, and they have come to Him and said, ''Is it lawful for a man to put away his wife for every cause?'' (Matt. 19:3). He talked their language, where they were. But when He gave the great overall picture, then He used these "exception" clauses (Matt. 19:9).

153. Church's Attitude Toward the Divorced

How do you treat divorced people in your church? Should they hold office or pastor a church? What about teaching a Sunday school class?

Dr. Sugden: This is how we treat divorced people in our church. We love them. We care for them. Did you know that "singles" is the most important ministry you can have today in any local church?

We don't accept them because they have done wrong. We accept them because in their wrong—if they have done wrong —they need help. So we began our singles work. Would you believe that it was the fastest growing thing in our church? From a start of seven, in a year, we have over a hundred. They came because they were hurting, and they found someone who would at least be gracious and kind to them, and say, "I sympathize with you. I want to help you."

And may I remind you that this is a growing problem, produced by the very nature of the society in which we live.

Mrs. Sugden: Now the question was about holding office.

Dr. Sugden: In my judgment, a divorced man cannot be a pastor. Now, this cuts across what many people think. I have a pastor friend whose wife walked out on him. What do you do in that situation? He was a fine pastor of a fine church. She simply walked out on him. The board of the church immediately met, because when she walked out, the pastor walked in and gave them his resignation.

They asked him, "What could you have done to save it? We have seen the situation, and we know what has happened. You are our pastor, and we are for you. And you care for us. We are going to keep you on as our pastor, if you will stay."

This man stayed on and ministered, and he has had a successful ministry. I honestly don't know what you do. We have problems today we never dreamed of forty years ago. What do we do with these situations?

But normally, the Word of God teaches that they cannot be deacons. In 1 Timothy 3:12 we learn that they must be the husband of one wife.

And then what about teaching? Does it say anything about that anywhere? No, it doesn't. So why can't they teach?

Mrs. Sugden and I picked up an old rule when we started out in college that says, "Where the Bible speaks, we speak; and where the Bible is silent, we're silent." And we're silent on that specific subject.

154. Church Membership for the Divorced

Should a divorced couple be accepted into church membership?

Dr. Sugden: Yes, why not? What would you do with them? Remember when the Lord Jesus stopped that day at Jacob's well? He really opened a "can of worms." Here was a woman who came to talk with Him. They talked, and she gave Him water to drink. He then revealed to this woman, who had been married five times, that she was living with a person who was not her husband. She had done all that. Do you know what Jesus did?

He revealed to her more than He did to any other person about Himself. He said, "I that speak unto thee am He [the Messiah]" (John 4:26).

And she said, "You're the Messiah!" She believed in Him. And would you believe it, she left and went back to the town and said, "Come, see a man who told me all things that ever I did" (John 4:29).

And the people came, and do you know what happened? "And many of the Samaritans of that city believed on Him for the saying of the woman . . ." (John 4:39).

155. Desertion

My son professed Christ at one time. He is now divorced, and I can't feel it is right for me to encourage or advise him to remarry. Yet I long to help him. Isn't it wrong for Christians to remarry when the wife is still living, although she has remarried? I know he needs to get right with the Lord first.

Dr. Sugden: What can he do with that marriage? He can do nothing, since his wife is remarried. In the case of Matthew 19, I believe that is the reason for divorce. I also believe (and this is a problem for which you don't just snap your fingers and pull an answer out of the air) that 1 Corinthians 7 teaches that if there is a case of desertion, which could involve many things such as abuse, that in that case the innocent party is privileged to remarry.

One of the best books on the subject is *Divorce and Remarriage* by Guy Duty. In the Old Testament the law says, "If a man find uncleanness in his wife" (it can't be sexual uncleanness, because she would be killed for that), he should divorce her, and she is free to marry another man. That throws a curve and a sinker at the same time, because the fellow at bat strikes out every time.

156. Divorced Serving in the Church

What is your view about divorced people holding church offices?

Dr. Sugden: There are two areas in the church where divorced people cannot serve: pastor and deacon.

Every once in a while, God breaks the mold and overrules. But I say this is the Word that God has given to us in these areas. When I was a boy growing up in our community, there was a Baptist pastor. He was the greatest man I ever heard as a boy. He taught us. He came to our little corner church frequently and taught us. Then he died. Do you know what happened after he died? Somebody went back into his life history and dug up the fact that this man had been divorced. Here was a man of God. He was something else.

So every once in a while, something happens that just tears you apart. But in the normal procedure, no pastor should be divorced and expect to continue in the ministry. The same is true of a deacon.

157. Does God Forgive Divorce?

Is a divorce the same as any other sin? And if so, will it be forgiven by God? Also, in view of the divorce rate today, do you think pastors should counsel young people more on this matter from a biblical viewpoint?

Dr. Sugden: There has never been a time when we have more conferences on the home than today. I could go to ten conferences a week, any week in the year, and get help for my marriage problems. We have never had a time when we have had more problems, so it must be saying something. Aren't you amazed that your parents ever survived without a conference?

If my mother and father had gone to a conference, they'd never have made it.

I think counseling is good, and I try to talk with young people. It's not easy to talk with them when they are in love. I don't think they hear a great deal. They love each other. They say, "Pastor, we'll make it."

So I think we have to do some preventive things. But after we have done that and something happens, what do we do? Then we collapse and say they have committed the unpardonable sin, and God will never forgive them? NO! They *can* be forgiven.

Divorce is not the unpardonable sin. We need to know that. In the world today we have to deal with these problems, and we can't just throw up our hands and say, "There is a divorced person: horrors."

When people make mistakes along the way, the church needs to be a caring community.

158. Exception Clause

In the recent book The Divorce Myth, *the author suggested that the exception clause regarding fornication is a direct reference to the Levitical law prohibiting incest. Please comment on this and share your opinion.*

Dr. Sugden: That view cannot be maintained. Probably the greatest writer on the gospel of Matthew is Broadus, who wrote a tremendous volume on the Book of Matthew. He deals with that section and with the exception clause. The exception means exactly what it says.

It means that if a husband or a wife is unfaithful, it is an occasion for divorce. You say, "Are there innocent parties?" I am talking about what the law says. I can't judge that. The innocent party in that case has a right to remarry. That's what we believe.

Pastor Wiersbe and I have worked together for years. Then we decided to write a book, which we did. We had to put down something that we knew people would read. When they read it, they would either agree or disagree with it. We would get "flack," or we would get approval. We put down what we believed, and Dr. Wiersbe and I believe the same.

But we're not alone. Literally hundreds of pastors take this stance, because we believe that adultery is a scriptural reason for divorce.

159. Fornication

According to Mark 10:4–12, Jesus said, "No remarriage at all or you will be committing adultery." Matthew 5:32 and Matthew 19:9 say, "except for fornication." A theory today says that this fornication refers to the Jewish betrothal period, because under the law (Lev. 20:10) adulterers were to be stoned. Therefore, it is wrong to divorce and remarry. What is your explanation of these and any other Scriptures on divorce?

Dr. Sugden: First, we will look at Mark 10:11, "And He said unto them, Whosoever shall put away his wife, and marry another, committeth adultery against her. And if a woman shall put away her husband, and be married to another, she committeth adultery" (Mark 10:11, 12).

Now notice. It says that they "put them away." This passage gives no reason for "putting away" to get somebody else. That's what some people say. It doesn't say that. It says "put them away."

When the Lord dealt with this subject in Matthew 19, He talked about "putting away" and then He gave the reason why they may be put away. Now the question was, "Could you put away your wife for any reason?" That is what Matthew said they asked. "Can I put away my wife for everything?" Jesus said, "No."

It is amazing. Someone goes back and says, "Well, I go back to the Old Testament and get my idea. You had better not go back to the Old Testament. Let me read it to you. When you read the Old Testament in Deuteronomy 24, it really throws you into convulsions. Here is what it says: "When a man hath taken a wife, and married her, and it come to pass that she find no favor in his eyes, because he hath found some uncleanness in her . . ." (Deut. 24:1).

Someone says, "Well, that was sexual unfaithfulness." It was not. If it were sexual unfaithfulness, she would have been dead. So it was not that. I have failed to find one commentary on the subject to explain what this uncleanness is. It doesn't say. It just says: ". . . hath found some uncleanness in her: then let him write a bill of divorcement, and give it in her hand, and send her out of his house. And when she is departed out of his house, she may go and be another man's wife" (Deut. 24:1, 2).

And she was the one that was wrong! That's right. That's what it says. That's the Old Testament. So you have to be very careful about going back under Jewish law and saying, "Well, this is the way it was."

And then the text goes on and says: "And when she is departed out of his house, she may go and be another man's wife. And if the latter husband hate her, and write her a bill of divorcement, and giveth it in her hand, and sendeth her out of his house; or if the latter husband die, which took her to be his wife; her former husband, which sent her away, may not take her again to be his wife . . . " (Deut. 24:2–4).

That's interesting. Now go to Matthew 19:3. "The Pharisees also came unto Him, tempting Him, and saying unto Him, Is it lawful for a man to put away his wife for every cause?"

Now that is exactly what Mark was talking about. Mark said, "Is it lawful for a man to put away his wife?" (Mark 10:2). Now they had added, "For every cause." Can you put her away? Suppose she burned the toast this morning. Suppose it happened yesterday too. Can he put away his wife? The Lord said, "No. She can't be put away for every cause." But then He did say that she can be put away if she has been unfaithful, if she has committed adultery. God gave two reasons for separation. First of all, unfaithfulness in the marriage; second, desertion.

You may disagree with me. But let me say this: I am sure that when God the Holy Spirit wrote the Word of God, He knew all that would happen in this generation. This has to be one of the most difficult questions we face today.

I know of women whose husbands have gone away and left them to care for four or five children. They work and slave. Then some self-righteous Christian comes along and says, "Isn't that terrible!" They pull their sanctified skirts around them and say, "Well, we just won't have anything to do with her."

What are you going to do with this great growing segment in society? You have to have some answers. And you have to consider the fact that God does somehow deal in grace. That He does forgive, and that He does restore. I'm talking with you out of my heart.

160. God's Will in Marriage

It was mentioned that God couldn't bless a couple if one of them was unsaved. How about the thought that a couple, being unequally yoked, would be in His will so that the unsaved man

*would become saved by the Christian influence of the partner,
thus blessing the marriage?*

Mrs. Sugden: Paul in 1 Corinthians 7 talks about that. Suppose one member of the family is saved and the other is not. If the unsaved one chooses to live with the saved one, they should stay together. This is because the saved one does have an influence on the unsaved.

Dr. Sugden: Hold it, dear. You see, a particular thing was happening in that early age. Everyone was a pagan. So here is a pagan couple. They are walking along the street one night, and they hear the apostle Paul preaching. They say, "Who is that? That's a great voice." They turn aside, and she is saved and he isn't.

Now, I believe, and I teach our young people in church, that a Christian fellow should marry a Christian girl. That is God's will. If they marry out of His will, that is not good. We have had many folk who have done that, and they have had lots of sorrows. But some have survived. Some have been saved, but the key fact is the will of God. That's what we are talking about. The will of God is that a saved man marry a saved lady. That's His will.

161. Marriage of an Unsaved Couple

*Should a minister refuse to marry a couple who are not
Christians?*

Dr. Sugden: Let's think about that. I had it drilled into me that this was the way you operated. So I followed that principle. You hear somebody else talk about this, and he says, "Oh, marrying two unsaved people is fine."

I started out that way. Then I discovered that across the city from me was a man who had pastored for years. All the people I refused went to him, and he married them. He was a better preacher and a better pastor than I was, and he knew more about the Word of God than I did. So I did some strong thinking about this.

Now, this will help you. Do you know that no pastor marries people because of the authority of the Word of God? I do not get my authority to marry people from the Bible. Paul didn't marry anyone. There is no record of the twelve apostles marrying anyone. The Lord Jesus visited a wedding, but it doesn't say that He married them. He was just there.

My authority to marry people is from the state. Now, I have to make the decision. Am I going to marry people that are unsaved? I have thought this through. Suppose an unsaved couple comes to me. I'm interested in them. I want to help them, and I say, "No, you're a couple of sinners. You don't have any business getting married, and I'll have nothing to do with you."

If a pastor thinks seriously, he says, "I have to make the decision myself." I can't turn to canon law. I have to turn to the Word of God. Does the Word of God give me authority to marry? No, it does not. The state gives me my authority, and the state tells me what I can and can't do. So I have to make a decision. I say, "I'm concerned about this couple, and I will marry them."

The Bible does not say that unsaved people are not to get married. It doesn't say anything about unsaved people. It does say something about saved and unsaved, or being unequally yoked together. That's a different thing. But when it comes to two lost people, it is a great opportunity to give them the gospel.

162. Punishment in Marriage for Pre-salvation Sexual Sin

Is it possible that God has withheld complete happiness from my marriage because of adulterous sin committed before salvation? We were married after we were saved.

Dr. Sugden: Never! You know, this bothers me sometimes when I hear people. They call and they cry on the phone about the sad situation of their little family. Maybe little Johnny is sick and they had to take him to the hospital. I go to the hospital and stand by the bed, and they say to me, "Oh, Pastor, what have we done to deserve this?"

I don't think that God is a monster waiting to jump on you.

Mrs. Sugden: No, He doesn't withhold happiness, does He?

Dr. Sugden: No.

Mrs. Sugden: We do that ourselves.

Dr. Sugden: But let me say this. The greatest thing that we can know as the people of God is the forgiveness of God, and honestly believe it. I have seen people go through life in utter misery. They are Christians, they are saved, and they say to me, "Pastor, I just can't believe that God has forgiven me."

God said He would. God doesn't lie. You can trust Him. When He says that He has forgiven you, He has forgiven you— free, full, and final forgiveness. Get up and go on. Isn't it wonderful that you can get up and go on. Be happy!

163. Remarriage of a Divorced Couple

Considering the divorce rate among Christians, would you remarry a man and woman who have been separated, profess to be Christians, and wanted to start over again?

Dr. Sugden: Oh, I certainly would! Some pastors won't, but really I think that that is one of the works we are involved in. We are involved in the great ministry of restoring people. We restore people to the Lord.

Men and women who have backslidden are out of fellowship, so we restore them. "Restore" is a great word; we restore people to each other. This is what we should do. We should always attempt this, and I do.

I am not a counselor. I have not felt that it was my call to leave the work of giving the good news to give good advice. God intended that the pastor be a dispenser of good news. One of the sad things about the ministry today is the pastor often spends more time giving good advice (and it may be good advice from God) than he does giving the good news of the Word of God. There should be balance in this, and sometimes it is all out of whack.

164. Separation

Is an unfaithful husband a "storm to be weathered," or can a Christian wife separate from the unfaithful Christian husband? If so, what does 1 Corinthians 7:10, 11 mean?

Dr. Sugden: When a wife or husband is unfaithful, the Word of God is explicit. I have talked with hundreds of pastors and boards of deacons. I always say to them, "Do you know what God's Word says?"

They say, "Well, we think we know."

I say, "I'm not asking what we think; I'm asking about what we know God's Word says." God's Word says that if a husband is unfaithful, or a wife is unfaithful, a divorce is granted and the one who is the innocent party has the right to remarry. That's exactly what the Word of God says. There is no question about it.

In fifty years I have spent hundreds of hours studying this subject. I do this because my pastor friends say, "We want somebody to say something." So I have something to say, and they may disagree. Now let me read Matthew 19:9. "And I say unto you, Whosoever shall put away his wife, except it be for fornication [or unfaithfulness], and shall marry another, committeth adultery: and whoso marrieth her which is put away doth commit adultery."

The Lord put in an exception. That's what He said. You say, "Well, Mark says it. Maybe he left that out, or maybe Luke. What's the difference?" Because the definitive portion of the Word of God is given in Matthew. You have other little brief statements about it, but this is the definitive one. Everyone who studies this will say the same thing.

Now let me say this, that no husband or wife is ever forced to separate in such a case. They know whether they are able to put the pieces back together.

165. Troubled Marriages

When referring to a number of Christian couples having marital problems, a person I know says that "there are marriages that should never have taken place." I feel this is a cop-out and rationalization to try and justify separation and divorce. Besides the fact that with God all things are possible, what response can we give them?

Dr. Sugden: It is sad to know that we need to have places of refuge for battered wives. It is hard for me to conceive, in the very nature of love and kindness and mercy and grace and compassion, that a man will be a wife-beater. I can't believe it. Yet there are hundreds of them, and wives need to have protection. This goes to show how far we have slipped in our morals and in our judgment today. I think that if a wife is beaten, God doesn't ask her to continue to live with this man.

The Word of God says, "If he be pleased to dwell." Apparently he is not pleased to dwell if he is misusing and beating her. I have tried to save homes and families. I don't know. What do you think?

Mrs. Sugden: I think God can take care of mistakes. All things are possible.

Dr. Sugden: God can forgive, but remember, there has to be willingness on both sides. There has to be a time when they meet and are absolutely willing to settle the difference, drop it, and start picking up the pieces again. If they are Christians, they have everything in their favor. If they will allow the Spirit of God to live in them and control them. But this takes teaching; it takes patience; it takes kindness. But homes can be saved. I have seen it, but it is often not with ease.

166. Unequal Yoke

A Christian girl is bound and determined to marry a non-Christian. Nothing can change her mind. How do we, as a family and friends, react?

Dr. Sugden: First of all, I would teach her that if you marry an unsaved person, you may have trouble with your father-in-law. You really will. You marry a child of the devil, and you will have trouble with your father-in-law.

We teach our people, but what they do with it is their responsibility. We communicate to our people that it is the will of God, and in the plan of God, for a believer to marry a believer and not to marry an unbeliever. We teach that. Now you see, you get yourself in an awful plight if you disobey.

I have a pastor friend, and everybody is always saved before they get married in his church. Then two months after that, he can't find them. The kids say, "Sure, I'll be saved to get married in the church." I don't think that's the way we operate. I think we need to teach them, and help them. If possible, we need to lead them to Christ—not to make a decision to be a Christian because this means they can have a church wedding. That should be taken care of long before the wedding. Our teaching is that we should marry believers, not unbelievers.

12
PRAYER

167. Fasting and Prayer

*Would you comment briefly on the significance and impor-
tance of fasting in relation to prayer?*

Dr. Sugden: Amazingly enough, there is very little written
on the subject of fasting. I would presume that the reason there
has been so little written on this subject is because in the Bible
there is very little said about it.

Paul's epistles are the standard rules of order for issues like
this, beginning with Romans. Of course, the gospels speak of
the Lord's disciples fasting. But very little is given.

I have a friend who came to a seminary and gave five lectures
for five days on fasting. The seminary paper had a little note in
it reporting, "Doctor So-and-So visited our campus and talked
about fasting, a subject which he apparently thinks is important." It didn't say anybody else did.

168. Prayer for the Sick

*With respect to the New Testament teaching about the elders
praying over the sick and anointing them with oil, please
comment on the relevance of this practice today. Who should
perform it? Is this a forgotten practice in today's church?*

Dr. Sugden: First of all, the teaching of anointing with oil is
found in James 5. This will help you. In the apostolic age,
different gifts were given to different people. They ceased
when the apostolic age ceased, about 100 A.D. when the canon
of Scripture was completed.

At that time Israel was set aside as a nation. At that time the
gospel was making its impact upon the whole world, and the
apostolic age closed. During the apostolic age God gave certain
things to the church, because they didn't have the completed
Bible. He gave them apostles. Apostles did special things as
evidence that they were apostles. Paul said: "Truly the signs of
an apostle were wrought among you in all patience, in signs,
and wonders, and mighty deeds" (2 Cor. 12:12). The same

things were spoken of the Lord Jesus. Those apostles did the same things that Jesus did.

169. Prayers of the Unsaved

Does God hear the prayers of the unsaved? Also what about Psalms 66:18, "If I regard iniquity in my heart, the Lord will not hear me"?

Dr. Sugden: There are really two questions here. Now let's be clear about this: those who are heard by the Father are His children. If you are a child of God by faith in Jesus Christ, He hears your prayer. If you are not a child of God, there is one prayer you offer which He will hear: "God, be merciful to me a sinner and save me." He always hears that prayer, and He answers it.

Now, the word from the psalmist is a word about believers. If there is something in my heart, a sin in my life, that I look upon with favor and hide and treasure, then God does not hear my prayer.

The way we take care of that is by the confession of our sin. The Book of 1 John was written to Christians, not to sinners.

In it we read: "If we confess our sins, He is faithful and just to forgive us our sins, and to cleanse us from all unrighteousness" (1 John 1:9).

If I, as a Christian, have done that which is wrong in the sight of God, the way He has of cleansing me is by my confession of my sin. Then he forgives.

170. How Much Time for Prayer

Exactly how much time a day should I spend in prayer?

Dr. Sugden: All the time you can; all the time you can! It depends on how much time you have. Don't spent time in prayer if you are working for somebody and you're supposed to be working. That is cheating; that is stealing.

I was talking with someone about the great men of God and their prayer lives. We talked about how these men prayed three hours. They got up at 4 o'clock in the morning and prayed.

My friend said, "Do you know what time they went to bed?"

I said, "No."

He told me, "They went to bed at six o'clock in the evening."

I think each of us has to make his own schedule. All of us

have the same amount of time—twenty-four hours a day. Time is the most valuable thing God gives to us.

I went to a conference not long ago. A fellow was teaching the pastors how to make use of their time. He had his day divided into 15-minute segments. I couldn't believe it. And this man was quite smart. I said to myself, "Dear Lord, that would be enough to drive one crazy."

However, you ought to have an orderly life. There's a hymn we sing, and in it is a little phrase that I love: "And let our ordered lives confess the beauty of Thy peace."

It's great to do that. But I think we ought to have a scheduled time—a time that we give to prayer. You may not have fifteen minutes. Some older people in rest homes can have hours a day to pray. Time is a precious thing. But we're just talking about you, so that you won't despair and say, "Oh, I read about Praying Hyde, and how he prayed. And I remember how Wesley prayed."

Yes, but Wesley and Hyde lived in a different world. They gave the amount of time to prayer that they could. And you should give the same proportion.

One of the great rules that God gave in the gathering of the manna was this: If a man had time to gather much, he never had any left over; but if he only had time for a little, he always had enough. Isn't that great! The same is true of prayer.

Some of you have to pray on the run. If you're on the road and you make calls, you can pray at stop lights. But don't close your eyes if you're driving. That's a bad habit, and I don't recommend it.

171. Pattern for Prayer

Mrs. Sugden said in the ladies' meeting that we pray to God the Father, through the Son, in the power of the Holy Spirit. Many Christians do not understand this. Could you give a word concerning this, and Scripture references if possible?

Mrs. Sugden: We pray to God the Father because that is what the Lord Jesus taught the disciples: "Our Father which art in Heaven" (Matt. 6:9). We read of the Son in John 14:13, and of the Spirit in Romans 8:26. Those are the references that apply.

Dr. Sugden: The Lord Jesus said: "And whatsoever ye shall ask in My name, that will I do, that the Father may be glorified in the Son" (John 14:13).

Mrs. Sugden: And the Spirit in Romans 8:26: "Likewise the

Spirit also helpeth our infirmities; for we know not what we should pray for as we ought: but the Spirit itself maketh intercession for us with groanings which cannot be uttered.''

Dr. Sugden: That is a good way to pray. Someone said, ''Do you object to people praying to Jesus?'' I don't find fault with people's prayers, but I think a procedure is taught in the New Testament, as Mrs. Sugden has indicated, that we pray to the Father, in the name of the Son, and in the energy of the Spirit of God. It is great to pray.

One of the most wonderful things we have in our city is that it is divided in two by trains. There are trains that seem like they have a thousand cars on them. I start out to do some calling, and the first thing I do is run into a train. I found early that I can sit there, wait, and say, ''Why is this train so long?'' or I can sit there and pray. It is a great place to pray, at trains, and God hears wherever we pray.

13
PROPHECY

172. Antichrist

In the end times a ruler, the man of lawlessness, is supposed to rise and bring a false peace to the earth. This man is presumably also coming from the Roman empire. How is communism going to submit to this man and worship him, when they think that they are Gog? And how can he bring peace since they (Gog) are supposed to march down upon Israel?

Dr. Sugden: If you put a map of the world on the wall, you will have east, west, north and south. That is what makes the day in which we live such a dramatic hour in the history of the world. Fourteen times in the Old Testament we read, "in the latter days." God pinpoints a time in history. He doesn't say it will happen in 1870 or 1990. He says, "the latter days," and tells what will happen. When you run those fourteen times through your computer, this is what you get.

Up at the north is a great nation, and the Word of God says that Russia is going to be on the move in the latter days. When I was a kid and studied geography—they call it social studies now—there were the funniest pictures of the Russians. They had pictures of old men and old horses and old sleds, and I thought, *Oh, Russia.* But when you see it today, it is one of the leading nations of the world, one of the great populations. There in the north is a leading power.

Then in the south there is a great power. There is a great power in the east. Do you know that no one can number the hoards of China? Their armies are as great right now as they are said to be in the Book of Revelation. So that's east.

And then you have a western federation of nations in Europe with England, Scotland, and Ireland (and you have that federation). Now these are the movements of nations in the latter days—the northern, southern, eastern and western. And all those nations right now have fallen into place and are waiting.

It is out of this western kingdom that the Antichrist is going to arise. He will be worshiped, but I don't think he will be worshiped in Russia. The Bible says they are going to fight against each other. That will make the battle of the last days, which is described in Ezekiel 38.

173. The Church and the Tribulation

What is the relation of the church to the tribulation? Will they go through it? Or will they escape it?

Dr. Sugden: I always think that if anyone really wants to go through the tribulation, the Lord may let him. No, I don't believe that! You say, "Pastor, are you a pre-tribulationist?" Yes, I am.

I am a pre-tribulationist, not because I was indoctrinated deeply in it. When I went to school (and Mrs. Sugden and I went together) they did one thing. They prepared preachers to preach. It was a great school.

If they had any position, it was an a-millennial position. You say, "Why were you there?" By design—by God's design. He took me there because He wanted me there. And He wanted her there. She taught school and put me through. She taught in the high school. I got a position as librarian.

We had thousands of volumes. Although they were an "a-millennial" school (they didn't believe in the Lord's pre-millennial return), they had everything in that library. Here I was, eager to learn, and I had all those books. I could never have bought them, and they were there at my fingertips. Every day I lived, I studied—and I studied about the prophetic Word.

Now I will give you some Scriptures that tell you why we take the pre-millennial position. I had to wrestle this out with the help of God, who wrestled for me. Here's why I believe as I do.

"But God commandeth His love toward us, in that while we were yet sinners, Christ died for us. Much more then, [He said if Christ died for us] being justified by His blood, we shall be saved from wrath through Him" (Rom. 5:8, 9).

Now someone comes along and says, "Yes, you use that verse. But don't you know that it is talking about the tribulations that we go through in life?"

Interestingly enough, we are not saved from tribulations in life.

We read, "In this world ye shall have tribulation" (John 16:33). But in Romans, Paul said we are going to be saved from tribulation. I don't think God contradicts Himself. He said there is a tribulation I shall be saved from. Now notice these verses:

> "For they themselves show of us what manner of entering in we had unto you, and how you turned to God from idols to serve the living and true God; and to wait for His Son from heaven, whom He raised from the dead, even Jesus, which delivered us from the wrath [and now he tells us when this wrath is going to be] to come" (1 Thess. 1:9, 10).

So we are going to be delivered from a coming wrath. That's what Paul said. I don't know how else you can deal with that verse. Now let's consider other verses: "But let us, who are of the day, be sober, putting on the breastplate of faith and love; and for a helmet, the hope of salvation. For God hath not appointed us to wrath . . ." (1 Thess. 5:8, 9).

God has not appointed me to wrath! Trouble, yes. I'm appointed to trouble as the sparks fly upward. I'm appointed to tribulation, because He said that in the world I will have tribulation. But He said He has not appointed us, as believers, to wrath, but to obtain salvation. The word for "salvation" used here has to do with the "completion" of our salvation. Our "completion" of salvation will be on the day we get our new bodies. And do you know what? I'll look better than I do now. "Oh," you say, "good. You can stand the improvement."

174. City of Babylon

Revelation 18 refers to the fall of Babylon. Do you agree that this is a prophetic reference? To whom do you feel this refers? Who is the Babylon of Revelation 18.

Dr. Sugden: The Book of Revelation is not mythological or allegorical. Revelation is the fulfillment of the prophetic movement of God. All that is going to take place in the tomorrows is included in this Book of Revelation.

At chapter 18 we come to the close of it all. John wrote:

> "After these things I saw another angel coming down from heaven, having great power; and the earth was lightened with his glory. And he cried mightily with a strong voice, saying, Babylon the great is fallen, and is become the habitation of devils, and the hold of every foul spirit . . ." (Rev. 18:1, 2).

Then he described what Babylon is. There are those who believe (and I think they have reason for this) that Babylon will be rebuilt. There is evidence that it is being planned at the very present moment. You see, it used to take years to build cities, but now we can build them almost overnight. They can move in with heavy equipment, and we would be shocked what can happen in a week in building a city. But there are many who believe that Babylon will be a literal city. Whatever it is, it is the center of every evil thing that happens.

Now there is one last word in Revelation 18:23, "And the light of a candle shall shine no more at all...."

Imagine a city with its lights out. Here is darkness. "...and the voice of the bridegroom and of the bride shall be heard no more..."

No more occasions of joy in this city. And then he says, "...for thy merchants were the great men of the earth; for by thy sorceries...." You read that and you say, "Well, I'm not interested in sorceries." You will be interested immediately, when you know that this is the Greek word for the drug culture. Whatever this city is, it is the center of all the drug culture of the world.

Do you know that when I was a teenager in high school, we never heard of drugs. We went through the years with no drugs. Now suddenly a whole new world is upon us. What a battle we have along our border taking care of the drugs that are pouring in.

But this city of Babylon will become the center of every evil thing. It will be the world capital of the drug culture. And you have a great move of God in the destruction of all that opposes Him. As Strat Shufelt so beautifully sings, "The conflict of the ages is upon us today." Never as great as today! It will culminate when the righteous God takes over and all evil, I think, finds its culmination in this city. Babylon—religious evil, social evil, financial evil—all these problems, and it is Babylon. So we are moving in that direction, and the destruction will take place.

175. Eschatology

Do you think eschatology is an important study for us today?

Dr. Sugden: Yes, it is. Now you say, "What in the world is eschatology? I don't know what the word means."

Eschatology is the doctrine of the last things. It is the doctrine of what is going to happen in the future. Many people are divided in their views about the last things.

I have discovered, as I read "Newsweek" and my business letters, that in the busy world of business where "dog eats dog" and men fight with each other for preeminence and prominence, there are no doubts about eschatology. Men believe that something cataclysmic is upon us.

For a long time I have taken the "Atomic Energy Bulletin." It is a valuable paper because it tells what is happening in the world of the atom and of energy. They have a clock and they move the hands. There was a time when it was ten minutes of twelve. When this year broke and the January issue came, the hands rested at three minutes to twelve. They say that we are nearing catastrophe.

When I read that bulletin and think of what is happening in our world today, and how the slip of a drug-overdosed man's finger could send us into an atomic war, I am overwhelmed. And businessmen out there who are looking at things, not as we see them with a view of Scripture, say as we say, "How much longer can we go on?"

For instance, a book was put out by the Massachusetts Institute of Technology on the subject of limits to growth. It is probably one of the greatest studies that has ever been done about how long we can go on living in this world the way it is. There will be a time when we will reach the limits. And when the limits are reached, that will be the end. That's what they think.

But we know the Word of God. And when we study the doctrine of eschatology, we believe that history is not a rudderless ship traveling through a tempestuous sea. We believe that history is under the direction of a sovereign God who knows all things from the beginning, and who moves everything toward a completed goal. And His goal is to put His Son on the throne of the universe. And He will do it!

You may ask, "Pastor, what do you believe, eschatologically?"

I believe that the coming of the Lord Jesus could be near at hand. As I read the Word of God, and I read what I see in the events that are taking place, I believe the Lord's return "draweth nigh."

I was thinking about this the other day as I read the 5th chapter of James. It says, "Woe unto you rich men." And it talks about silver and gold. I never thought about it. Suddenly gold and silver are big items. Our great problems today are the problems that on which God focuses in James 5: the problem of capital and labor; the problem of men who say that they have not gotten what they deserve. I don't know whether they have or not. I only know that it is a fulfillment of what's in the Bible.

I like what one newspaper reporter wrote. "I don't know anything about the Scriptures, but I know one thing—I smell the 'wind-up' in the air." There are times when you go outside and sniff, and you say, "It smells like a storm." You can sift out the smells. This man said, "I smell the wind-up." And that's eschatology.

It's a great study. Don't neglect it. It is something that stirs you when you study about what God is doing, about what He has done, about what He is yet to do, and where you fit into the totality of the plan and purpose of God.

176. Jews in Prophecy

Are the Jews in Israel a prophetic sign?

Dr. Sugden: I believe so. But for some people, the only thing they see in their Bibles is prophecy. We have the conviction that you cannot understand the movement of God in history, or what God is doing today, unless you become in some measure a student of the prophetic Word of God. God has a plan for the nations.

What is that plan? It is not that the United States will be the Kingpin of all nations! You could declare. You could guess. But the Word of God gives the prophetic plan for the nations.

God has a prophetic *plan for Israel* that began in Genesis 12, and that plan has not changed. Israel is still God's nation. The land of Palestine belongs to Israel. God gave it to them. It does not belong to the P.L.O. It does not belong to the Arabs. God has a plan, and Israel will be back in that land. It will become the center of the reign of Christ in the millennium. That's what the Word of God says about Israel.

A couple who had recently come to the Lord were asked, "What was the greatest evidence that there is God?" Do you know what they answered? I think it was good. They said, "The evidence of the Jew in the world."

Someone said of the Jews, "They tried to kill them with work, they built gallows for them, they have done everything. Even Hitler had his ovens, but they have never been able to exterminate them."

God told them He would preserve them, and He has kept His promise!

God has a *plan for the church.* When we started our ministry, the only real thing that was on the move and being taught extensively was that the world was getting better. Finally, the kingdom of God would come, and the church would bring in the kingdom. We'd go to meetings and people would pray, "Oh, Father, bring in your kingdom." They thought the church was bringing in the kingdom. They hadn't the foggiest notion what the kingdom was all about.

The church is not bringing in the kingdom. The church is not going to bring universal peace. The church is the people God has saved out of the world for His name. When that process is completed, He will take them out. "Hallelujah, we shall rise," as we sing.

177. New Heaven

Is the heaven where Christ's church will live eternally going to be established on the new earth? Will this occur after Jesus' 1000-year reign on earth? Please clarify.

Dr. Sugden: According to Revelation 21, John saw a new heaven and a new earth. Then he saw the Holy City coming down from God out of heaven.

I think you have in Revelation 21 and 22 a picture of the eternal state. And in that eternal state, I am convinced, heaven and earth will be closely tied together.

Have you ever read in Revelation 21 about the nations? Just think, in that eternal state there will be nations! It talks about the nations three times in that chapter, so there is a very close tie. But the church, I believe, will be a special people of God through all eternity. We will be special in the ages to come.

178. The Millennial Reign

Who are the people who will reign with Christ during the millennium?

Dr. Sugden: Look at Revelation 20:4, "And I saw thrones, and they sat upon them, and judgment was given unto them: and I saw the souls of them that were beheaded for the witness of Jesus, and for the Word of God, and which had not worshiped the beast, neither his image, neither had received his mark upon their foreheads, or in their hands: and they lived and reigned with Christ a thousand years."

Here is somebody that is going to live and reign with Christ 1000 years, and then you have the problem of the millennium. You say, "You believe in the millennium?"

I certainly do. I would have an awful time taking care of some thirty passages in Isaiah that refer to a time when something is going to happen on this earth that has never happened on earth before.

When is that going to be? You have to fit the Scripture passages together somehow. My greatest teacher was a brilliant man by the name of William Edward Biederwolf. He was a great preacher and scholar. He wrote a book entitled, *The Millennium Bible*. It didn't sell well, so after he died they changed the name to *The Second Coming Bible Commentary*. It was amazing how he put together all the passages that relate to a time when the Lord Jesus is going to reign. Paul said that we will reign with Him. I believe that all members of the body of Christ will share in this reign of Christ upon the earth.

You don't have to believe it to go to heaven, but it will be a nice surprise when you get there to find out I am right.

179. Pre- and Amillennial Teaching

Please explain the difference between the premillennial and the amillennial teaching. Does it matter which we believe?

Mrs. Sugden: Yes, it does.

Dr. Sugden: To explain it in simple language, premillennial teachers of the Word of God believe that the days in which we live will increase in wickedness. "Perilous times shall come," Paul said to Timothy. Then the Lord will come in a day of unprecedented violence and wickedness upon the earth, and He will take out the church.

Then there will come a tribulation period on the earth. After that, the millennium will come. We will return with our Lord to reign. This is premillennial teaching.

The amillennial teaching is that all the promises made to Abraham, Isaac, and Jacob—and to the Jews—are fulfilled in the church. There is no millennium.

We do not fight with those who disagree with us. We make no apology. We happen to be premillennial believers. I have read every book that I could, and I have tried to study and be honest with my people. When someone comes to me and says, "Pastor, I disagree with you," I never collapse and say, "Oh, horrors."

I think we have to have reasons for believing as we do. This does not mean we are to close our eyes to other folk who say they believe other ways. This is the premillennial position.

180. Rapture of the Church

Will the rapture of the church occur before or after the Great Tribulation?

Mrs. Sugden: It will occur before. I always say, "If you want to go through the tribulation, it is okay with me, but I'm not going through it." I say the same thing about eternal security. "If you don't want to believe that you are secure when you are born again, it is all right with me." You are not going to take the joy out of my life. If you want to go through suffering all your life, go ahead.

Dr. Sugden: Go ahead and struggle. Don't enjoy your salvation. Let me just say a word about the Lord's return. We don't quarrel over great doctrines. We affirm them. We have no time for quarreling in our house of God. We affirm what we believe, and the problem will not be with me. It will be with the Word of God. So it is my responsibility, as best I can, to expound the Word of God to my people. I do so in such a way that they too will trust and believe, if the doctrines are sound. And they are.

But when it comes to the Lord's return, our personal conviction is that the Lord is going to come before the tribulation. He is coming for His church. He will remove his church. As I say, it isn't something we fight about. But I think that if someone would sit down with me for about an hour with the Word of God, and just take the scriptures—the Book of Revelation—we would agree. It is amazing to note that in the first three chapters of Revelation, the church is referred to nineteen times. All of a sudden the church is not heard of again until the 19th chapter.

What has happened to the church? Something must have happened to it. Battles and wars against the church are not mentioned. Great battles are going on, but the church has suddenly disappeared from chapter 4. It has to be somewhere, and we think that the church is in heaven. John represents the church in Revelation 4:1 when he says, "After this I looked, and behold, a door was opened in heaven."

181. Rebuilding Babylon

What evidence is there for the rebuilding of Babylon?

Dr. Sugden: As far back as a hundred years ago there was talk about rebuilding Babylon. Dr. James M. Gray, who was the president of the Moody Bible Institute, wrote a book called, *A Primer of Prophecy.* In that book he has given a chapter to the rebuilding of Babylon.

Many movements are going on today to rebuild the city. There is a great stirring among the nations about Babylon. This is not prophecy, this is what nations are doing. I think even Russia has made a generous contribution to have Babylon rebuilt.

There is evidence in the world. There is also the evidence in the Word of God. I believe that the Book of Revelation, as you read it, indicates that it is possible that Babylon will be rebuilt.

One of the fantastic things said about it is found in Revelation 18:2, "And he cried mightily with a strong voice, saying, Babylon the great is fallen, is fallen, and is become the habitation of devils."

Babylon will be the demon center of the world, says the Book of Revelation. So it is possible.

Some think it is a reference to the city of Rome. But I feel, that rather than a reference to the city of Rome today, it probably speaks of a rebuilt city, where Babylon once stood.

182. Salvation During the Tribulation

I am wondering about the great multitude before the throne, as mentioned in Revelation 7:9 and 14. Were these numbers of Gentiles saved out of the tribulation before or after the rapture of God's people?

Dr. Sugden: Chapters 1, 2 and 3 of Revelation are pretribulation experiences. At the close of chapter 3 the church, which is mentioned nineteen times in chapters 2 and 3, is not mentioned again until Revelation 19. So between the close of chapter 3 until chapter 19 there is no mention of the church.

The great multitude of people in the 7th chapter are men and women out of every tongue and nation on earth. They are identified as "they which came out of great tribulation, and have washed their robes, and made them white in the blood of the Lamb" (Rev. 7:14).

They have come out of the great tribulation, so they are tribulation saints. You say, " I didn't know people were going to be saved in the tribulation." But remember, great multitudes in this world today have never heard the gospel.

Multitudes in the United States can tune in any Lord's Day morning and hear anything they want on television. They can get great gospel preaching as well as other programs. I'm glad for gospel preaching. I'm glad for Jerry Falwell and Richard De Haan. I'm glad for these men who give the gospel, but in spite of this, in the United States are millions of people who have never heard the gospel. Those are the ones who will be saved during the tribulation.

Now you say, "How do you know that?" Second Thessalonians 2:10-11 says that if a man has the opportunity to hear and doesn't believe, when the tribulation comes, he will be given strong delusion. This is so that he might believe the lie—not a lie, but the lie.

183. Six Sixty-six (666)

During the past 2 or 3 years, the 666 configuration has appeared as a prefix on some government form numbers, as well as some credit card systems and international monetary forms. Do you believe that this is simply a coincidence, or is it part of a great sinister plot that is slowly forming through the world?

Dr. Sugden: I read somewhere that all the license plates in Israel had "666" on them. I tried to see if that were true when I was in Israel, and I saw no license plates with "666."

You have to have numbers on credit cards. I am rather cynical about looking at things like that and saying that it is one of the signs of the times. The number 666 can be added up and you can get anything. I have thrown away many books on the number "666." I have a friend, now in heaven. He said that he had buried six antichrists, so you can always have things like that.

The number six is just short of seven.

Mrs. Sugden: The number six is the number of man, isn't it?

Dr. Sugden: Yes, and seven is the number of completeness in the Word of God. Six is the number of man; it is short of God. Man falls short in all his plans, in all his purposes, and in everything he does. He is always short of God's ideal, which is seven.

14

SABBATH OR
THE LORD'S DAY

184. Holy Day

I would like your comment on keeping the Lord's day holy. There is much discussion in our church about what is acceptable and unacceptable behavior for Sundays.

Dr. Sugden: You will see immediately that I am dated, because we were brought up in an era when the Lord's day was a special day. Our workload was minimal on Sunday on the farm. My father would not allow any work to be done on the Lord's day.

Our cattle and horses had to be fed. That was permissible, but outside of that we did no work. I was born and raised in an area that has sports, but my father would never allow us to play any sport on the Lord's day.

I am bothered these days, because I think we have lost something of the wonder of the Lord's day. I believe it could mean more to us. But I am always grateful to find my people in the house of God on the Lord's day, when we have the opportunity to worship and to praise and to have fellowship.

I think the Lord's day should be a day when we enjoy fellowship with God and with our fellow believers, and when we do those things that promote Christian fellowship and Christian faith. It should be rather an enjoyable experience. We ought to make it that way. It would probably help if we could keep other activities at a minimum. But this is easier to talk about than it is to do.

Mrs. Sugden: Today all the stores are open.

Dr. Sugden: There was a day when we moved to lovely London (Ontario). I remember the Lord's day in London. It was so quiet. In those morning hours I could look out, or stand in our back yard, and hear the church bells ringing. All the theaters and sports activities were shut down.

Mrs. Sugden: But that is not true anymore.

Dr. Sugden: No, it isn't true now. We have lost a great deal, but there is no use in turning back and saying, "Well, we long for the good old days." We can be saved in the midst of crowds and in the midst of noise and confusion. But I think that the Christian should always find the Lord's day a time for worship, a time for prayer, and a time for his own devotional life. I think that should be part of his Lord's day.

Mrs. Sugden: I think you have to watch it too, for children. Don't make it a day that they hate. I think it is very important that you do something with your children so that they would look forward to the Lord's day.

Don't make yourselves and your children slaves of what you believe and what you do. I think it is important that children enjoy the Lord's day. Make it a very special day, some way, for the children.

Dr. Sugden: I always felt sorry for my mother, on the Lord's day, but it turned out for our benefit because we always had jello and bananas. That was great!

Mrs. Sugden: We are not under the law of the sabbath. That is one thing we have to remember.

185. Israel and the Sabbath

What about the sabbath?

Dr. Sugden: A Saturday sabbath was not given to the church of Jesus Christ. We are in a new economy. The old covenant relates to Israel; the new covenant relates to the church of Jesus Christ. There is a tremendous difference between them.

When Jews are saved, they become Christians and move out from under that old covenant into a new covenant. Now you say, "How do you know that the sabbath belongs to Israel?" The reason that I know is because God said it, and when God says it, I can't do anything but accept it.

Look at Exodus 31:12. I never get boisterous about this when I talk with people. I quietly read it and say, "Now this is what God says." "And the Lord spake unto Moses, saying, Speak thou also unto the children of Israel . . ."

To whom did God say Moses was to speak? The children of Israel? Isn't it amazing that it doesn't say "speak unto the church"? It says, "Speak unto the children of Israel." Notice what it says: "Speak thou also unto the children of Israel, saying, Verily My sabbaths ye shall keep: for it is a sign between Me and you throughout your generations . . ." (Exod. 31:13).

God said, "It is a sign that I have given to you as a nation, and as a people throughout all your generations." The Bible doesn't say it is going to be the church—the sabbath never was to the church.

Now, you shall keep the sabbaths throughout your generations, ". . .that ye may know that I am the Lord that doth sanctify you. Ye shall keep the sabbath therefore; for it is holy unto you: every one that defileth it shall surely be put to death. . ." (Exod. 31:13, 14).

Do you know any place where anyone is put to death today for breaking the sabbath? That's what it says. If you accept the sabbath, then you have to accept this.

I'll never forget my friend, Dr. Harry Ironside. He went into an adventist church one day. It was a cold morning. Everybody was seated, and Dr. Ironside walked in with his big old coat on. He pulled his collar around his neck. An usher came along and asked, "Would you like to put your coat on the rack?"

"No," said Dr. Ironside, "it would be too cold." Another usher asked him the same question, and Dr. Ironside said, "Isn't this an adventist church?" They said "Yes." He asked, "Aren't you keeping the sabbath?"

"Yes," they said.

"Oh, then you'll not have any fire this morning." But they had both boilers fired up. They were not keeping the sabbath. The law said, "If you build a fire on the sabbath, if you break the sabbath, you all will be killed." They don't obey that. How do you explain this away?

Now look at verse 17: "It is a sign between me and the children of Israel for ever. . ." So when the children of Israel keep the sabbath today, they are right. Many of them do, and they keep it so rigidly that it is almost terrifying. They are not right in that they do not believe that the Messiah has come. But if I were a Jew and believed as they believe, I would keep the sabbath.

186. The Lord's Day

What day is the Lord's day?

Mrs. Sugden: The first day of the week.

Dr. Sugden: By the way, we have almost lost that, because we don't teach about the Lord's day. People come to me in pastors' meetings, and they dare say to me, "Why do you believe in the Lord's day?"

They should be answering the questions for their people instead of asking me questions about the Lord's day. The Lord's day was the day of our Lord's resurrection. He rose from the dead on the first day of the week. The Holy Spirit of God came and baptized the believers into one body on the day of Pentecost, on the first day of the week. The early church met on the first day of the week.

You ask, "How do you know?" Because that's what the Bible says. They met on the first day. When Paul wrote to the Corinthians, he said they should not forget the offerings when they met on the first day of the week (1 Cor. 16:1, 2). A few churches will forget the offering, but they are urged to take up offerings on the first day of the week.

This may be a hard passage from the Book of Revelation. But it always thrills me when I think of John, as they put him in that little motor boat and somebody drove it. It went bouncing over the waves and pushed its nose up against the Isle of Patmos. An aged man stepped out upon that Isle, and it was almost a fortress. He was held hostage. Think of it! He was a hostage on Patmos when the Lord's day came, and he said, "I was in the Spirit on the Lord's day" (Rev. 1:10).

Today we would be in our cars or in our boats on the Lord's day. He was in the Spirit on the Lord's day.

Mrs. Sugden: It is the first day of the week.

Dr. Sugden: That's right, the first day of the week.

187. The Sabbath Day

When was the sabbath changed?

Mrs. Sugden: The sabbath has never changed.

Dr. Sugden: Now I will tell you why it wasn't changed. These are truths that we know, but we don't often think about them. We commonly use the word "sabbath" for the day we worship. It bothers me. It bothered me more when I was a kid beginning to preach, because one of my men in our first congregation would pray and say, "Now Father, bless us on this sabbath day."

I said, "Well, I'll correct it," so I preached a sermon and he came to me afterwards and said, "It was a great sermon, Pastor.

I certainly appreciate the truth.'' I had told him that the sabbath was not the Lord's day. So the next time he prayed just like he had prayed before. He didn't change a bit.

But the sabbath was given to Israel. The strongest word I have to give is found in Exodus 31. The sabbath didn't change, as Mrs. Sugden said. There was a new day for a new age. If you go to Israel, walk the streets of Jerusalem, and get in certain sections, you will meet those Jews who meticulously keep the sabbath today as they kept it back in the day our Lord was here. And they are right in doing it. If I were a Jew this morning, I would keep the sabbath day because I would be an orthodox Jew. I would keep the sabbath because God gave me that as a special day.

But I am a Christian, and I keep the Lord's day. He gave me that day. It was the day that the Lord Jesus rose from the dead; it was the day when the church was born. The church was born on the day of Pentecost, which was the day after the sabbath, the first day of the week.

The early church kept the first day of the week. In Acts 20, Paul stayed a whole week in a certain place so he would be there for the Lord's day when they had their services. And 1 Corinthians 16, simply says that you gather together your offerings upon the first day of the week.

Now this is the Sabbath: "And the Lord spake unto Moses, saying, Speak thou also unto the children of Israel . . ." (Ex. 31:12, 13). I put a big circle around that so even if I had misty optics, I could see it.

"Speak thou also unto the children of Israel, saying, Verily My sabbaths ye shall keep: for it is a sign between Me and you throughout your generations, that ye may know that I am the Lord that doth sanctify you.

Ye shall keep the sabbath therefore: for it is holy unto you: every one that defileth it shall surely be put to death: for whosoever doeth any work therein, that soul shall be cut off from his people.

Six days may work be done; but in the seventh is the sabbath of rest, holy to the Lord: whosoever doeth any work in the sabbath day, he shall surely be put to death.

Wherefore the children of Israel shall keep the sabbath, to observe the sabbath throughout their generations, for a perpetual covenant" (Ex. 31:13-16).

You just can't escape this passage. You can juggle words. But if the Bible is a nose of wax that you can twist to fit your theories, then it is of no value at all. God was talking here to Israel. Now notice:

"Wherefore the children of Israel shall keep the sabbath . . . for a perpetual covenant.

It is a sign between Me and the children of Israel forever: for in six days the Lord made the heaven and earth, and on the seventh day He rested, and was refreshed" (Ex. 31:16, 17).

Isn't is amazing that when you read the Bible, you say, "Something struck me as you were reading that, Pastor." What was it? There is a battle going on. I have good friends on both sides, and I love them both. But some of them say, "Well, creation came in six ages of thousands of years in an age."

Wouldn't you like to be right? I'll help you to be right. God was not talking about creation here—only in the sense that He brings it in. He was not giving an exposition of creation, but He did say something here about it. He said that it was in six days that the Lord created heaven and earth, and on the seventh day He rested.

Mrs. Sugden: In the New Testament, you will find that all of the principles of the ten commandments are given in the New Testament as principles (not as laws, but as principles) except one: "Remember the sabbath and keep it holy." That was not repeated even as a principle in the New Testament.

15
SALVATION

188. Age of Accountability

Do the Scriptures indicate that children are not accountable until a certain age? What biblical basis is there for the belief that infants go to heaven when they die?

Dr. Sugden: I would suggest that you study with great care Romans 5:20, "Where sin abounded, grace did much more abound." Study the "much mores" in Romans 5.

I believe that the great chapter on this question is Matthew 18. The Lord Jesus called a child to Himself, set him in the midst of the disciples, and said: "Except ye be converted, and become as little children, ye shall not enter into the kingdom of heaven" (Matt. 18:3). What was He saying? He was saying if you are to enter heaven, you need to become like a little child. You need have a child's attitude, a child's cleanness, a child's trust. So I think He was saying that little children go to heaven.

The best word on this, of course, is in 2 Samuel 12. I point this out to you on the death of David's little child. When David's child died, the neighbors all wondered what David would do. They said, "What will he do? Will he collapse?" He had been in the office, and then he came home and found that the little child was dead. David arose and washed himself. Then we read:

> "... and changed his apparel, and came into the house of the Lord, and worshiped...
>
> Then said his servants unto him. What thing is this that thou hast done? Thou didst fast and weep for the child, while it was alive; but when the child is dead, thou didst rise and eat bread.
>
> And he said, While the child was yet alive, I fasted and wept: for I said, Who can tell whether God will be gracious to me, that the child may live?
>
> But now he is dead, wherefore shall I fast? Can I bring him back again? I shall go to him..." (2 Sam. 12:20–23).

Where did David go? Heaven! How do you know he went to heaven? He said he did. In Psalm 23:5, he said, "I will dwell in the house of the Lord forever." And he said, "My little baby has gone to heaven, and I will go to be with my little child. I can't bring the child back, but I can go where the child is.'' Isn't that wonderful?

I love to preach on this in funerals for little children. Just think, when a little child goes through the door of heaven, he always leaves the door ajar so Dad and Mon can get in. Isn't that wonderful? It is just a great sermon for children.

Mrs. Sugden: Back in the Old Testament, the age of accountability was twenty. The redemption money did not have to be paid until they were twenty years of age.

Dr. Sugden: That seems old to us today. But all of the folk that came out of the land of Egypt with Moses that were above 20 years of age, all the folk that murmured and complained and sinned along the way, every one of them died. It is amazing!

189. Assurance of Salvation

Some people say we cannot know that we are saved. We can only hope that we are saved. How does one answer them about the Christian's definite assurance of salvation?

Dr. Sugden: Read 1 John. It was written ''that we might know.'' Our salvation is dependent entirely on what God has done, what God has said. It doesn't depend on emotions. Salvation is a fact.

There was an hour when God put His Son upon the tree. Christ became sin for us. He put away the sin of the world. It has been settled forever—forever! He did it once. That's all He had to do. Only one cross, one death, one sin-bearer; and He put away the sin of the world.

The news of the gospel is this: ''He that believeth on the Son of God *hath* everlasting life'' (John 3:36). I'll never forget dealing with a lad one day about the Lord Jesus. I said to him, ''Do you believe that Jesus died for you?'' I gave him that verse, and he said, ''Yes, I do.''

I then said, ''Now tell me, it says that he that believeth on the Son of God, Jesus Christ, hath life. Could you tell me what that means?''

He said, ''You've got it.''

Who said I was to have life? God did. Would God lie? No, God won't lie. Then it is the *fact* that makes the difference.

To teach this, turn to John ''that you may know'' (1 John 5:13). Mark the word *know* through the book of 1 John, and you will have it. He says that "we have passed from death unto life." We know that we have.

190. Babies at the Rapture

At the rapture, what will happen to babies and young children, especially those little ones of born-again parents? What about little ones in a household where only one parent is a believer?

Mrs. Sugden: I think all babies will go to heaven—all babies.

Dr. Sugden: Yes, of course. Let me just say a little word about babies. I don't want to say a big word—just a little word. If babies go to heaven when they die—and they do—they'd certainly be raptured.

191. Conformed to His Image

If at salvation we are ready to go to heaven, what is the meaning of Romans 8:29, "conform to the image of His dear Son"? I have understood that God uses the trials of life to do this.

Dr. Sugden: I believe the trials of life are used to do this. That's what it says in Romans 8:29. But look first at Romans 8:28, "And we know that all things work together for good to them that love God, to them who are called according to His purpose." And then Paul wrote: "For whom He did foreknow, He also did predestinate to be conformed to the image of His Son..." (Rom. 8:29).

All the experiences of our lives, whether they are good or evil, come to shape us and to conform us. Even so, we will not be fully conformed to the image of His Son until the day we see Him. That will be the final touch. John said: "Beloved, now are we the sons of God, and it doth not yet appear what we shall be: but we know that, when He shall appear, we shall be like Him..." (1 John 3:2).

It will happen in that day. That's when we will be conformed. That will be the final work, but everything He does of good or sorrows—everything that He drops into the crucible of life's experience, into the mixing bowl of our lives—He does to shape us.

Mrs. Sugden: But that does not prepare us for heaven.

Dr. Sugden: Salvation prepares us for heaven. The "being conformed" prepares us to live here. And it helps us to grow through trials, because other people can enjoy us.

192. Election and Security

Why is it that in 2 Peter 1:10 we are urged to "give diligence to make your calling and election sure," when Calvinists claim eternal security for those whom God has elected for salvation?

Mrs. Sugden: You have to make your election sure by believing in Jesus Christ as Savior. It's that simple. Then you are elected.

Dr. Sugden: You will never get elected if you don't run. So you must "run" in some measure. Remember, "faith comes by hearing, and hearing by the Word of God." But Peter is not talking in this passage so much about the assurance of our own hearts, even though it is an assurance when we see fruit and we see evidence. But we don't look to evidence and to fruit—we look to Him.

Our calling and election, however, are made definite as the evidence is beheld. I am talking now about the life that other people see. They recognize that something has happened in your heart. I think that is the meaning of it, and most commentators agree.

193. Eternal Security

Would you please comment on eternal security—"once saved, always saved"?

Mrs. Sugden: Look at John 14: "And I will pray the Father, and He shall give you another Comforter, that He may abide with you forever" (John 14:16).

The Holy Spirit dwells in us forever. He doesn't leave us when we are born again. Let me give you some more verses:

"My sheep hear My voice, and I know them, and they follow Me: And I give unto them eternal life: and they shall never perish, neither shall any man pluck them out of My hand.

My Father, which gave them Me, is greater than all: and no man is able to pluck them out of My father's hand" (John 10:27-29).

Sometimes people profess to know Christ. But there's a great deal of profession that is not possession. There's a big difference between profession and possession. Many who profess to be saved may not really be saved. John, in his epistle tells us, "They went out from us, but they were not of us: for if they had been of us, they would no doubt have continued with us; but they went out, that they might be made manifest that they were not all of us" (1 John 2:19).

I know the background is doctrinal. David said in Psalm 51:12, "Restore unto me the joy of my salvation...". He did not say "restore unto me my salvation," but "restore unto me the *joy* of my salvation." Salvation was not lost; just its joy.

People come back by quoting Matthew 24:13, which says, "But he that shall endure to the end, the same shall be saved." That is always thrown at me. They don't know what it means. Christ is not talking about salvation here but about the tribulation. You endure to the end if you can keep from getting killed during the tribulation.

If you're not a dispensationalist, if you do not believe in the dispensations, your interpretation will be faulty. I know people get away from the Lord and backslide. God chastens His children, just like you chasten your children. If they are really saved, they will come back.

Dr. Sugden: You are so right, dear.

194. Exact Date of Salvation

If a person has no recollection as to the day, month, or even year that he was saved, do you think that salvation really took place?

Mrs. Sugden: I can't remember the day and the month and the year that I was saved, but I am saved.

Dr. Sugden: I think it would be nice for us to be able to say, "Well, it was 9:30 on a Tuesday evening on such and such a day." But you may not be able to do that. The great question is, "Do you know you are saved right *now*?" Do you have an answer to that question? Are you saved today?

Some of you were saved when you were young. I have always been shocked when I read of a great man like Matthew Henry, who was saved when he was five years of age. Many great men in history have been saved when they were six years of age. I would presume that as they reach the age of 70 or 75, they might not remember the exact details. But I think the greatest need for you today is to know that you are saved, and to be able to say, "I know that I have believed in Jesus Christ. I trust Him as my Savior, and I belong to God."

I remember the night when I was saved. I'm glad that I can

174 / What Does the Bible Say About . . . ?

remember that night, but I was nineteen years of age. But the all-important thing is, "Do you *today* know Christ in your heart as your Savior?"

Can you say, "My hope is built on nothing less than Jesus' blood and righteousness"? I hope you can.

Mrs. Sugden: You can know it by His Spirit witnessing with your spirit that you are children of God.

195. The Gospel

It tells us in 1 John 2:24 to "let that abide in you which ye have heard from the beginning." What was it we heard in the beginning?

Dr. Sugden: The gospel. If you are saved, you heard it first in the gospel. That is the only way you are saved.

When I was a little kid, we went to a country church. I always wondered, after I grew older, why I had not heard the message then. The night I was saved, I went back over my life. I wondered why, in the little church on the hill, somebody had not talked with me about the Lord Jesus. We learned the Ten Commandments, and I'm sure they were great. But no one talked about the Lord Jesus to us, and that is the word that you "heard at the beginning."

When you hear that word, it abides in you. You never lose the wonder of that word of the gospel that reached in and saved your soul. When you come to the close of life, you will be singing, "Amazing Grace." "Through many dangers, toils and snares" is the amazing grace of God that we heard in the gospel.

196. Hardened Heart

A man we know rejected Christ years ago, and now he says he cannot receive Christ as His Savior because he made his choice years ago. What would you say to him?

Dr. Sugden: I feel that there probably comes a time in the life of an individual when a rejection is made that seals that individual's destiny. I have heard this, and am inclined to believe it. There comes a time in life, after consistent and constant rejection, that "he, that being often reproved, hardeneth his neck, shall suddenly be destroyed, and that without remedy" (Proverbs 29:1).

So I think there is a possibility of one resisting, hardening his heart. But I would dare say, in the light of the grace of God, that such occurrences would be few.

197. Household Salvation

The Lord has promised us that our whole household will be saved. If the Lord should come today and our loved ones are not saved, what will happen? Will there be an instant conversion? It is the only thing that makes me fear the Lord's second coming.

Dr. Sugden: You are thinking of Acts 16, where the jailor cried out to Paul, "What must I do to be saved?" (v. 30). Paul's answer was: ". . . Believe on the Lord Jesus Christ, and thou shalt be saved, and thy house" (Acts 16:31).

Many folk take this to be a promise that not only will we be saved, but our household will be saved as well. Your house will be saved, naturally, if they have personal faith in Jesus Christ. That is how they will be saved. If in the plan and program of God He has included them, they will be saved before the rapture.

I believe the church will leave when it is completed. The Lord's body, His church, will leave. If they are included in the Body, they will leave. They will be saved before that day comes.

198. Loss of Salvation

Does the Bible teach a person can give up his salvation? What about Romans 12:17-20; John 15:1-6; 2 Peter 2:1-4, 21, 22, and many other scriptures?

Dr. Sugden: Let me say that the passages quoted are talking about fellowship and service and fruit—not root. There is a difference between "root" and "fruit." Many Christians have lives that are apparently fruitless, but if they are saved, they cannot lose their salvation.

When I was saved, I began to think through the Word of God without the aid of seminary or Bible school. You just can't read through the Word of God without concluding that what God begins to do in us is an eternal thing. You see, He gave us salvation. If He takes it away, He didn't really give it to us, did He? What are you going to do with verses like this:

"My sheep hear my voice, and I know them, and they follow Me: And I give unto them eternal life; and they shall never perish, neither shall any man pluck them out of My hand.

My Father which gave them Me, is greater than all: and no man is able to pluck them out of My Father's hand" (John 10:27-29).

Then think of a word like this: "He which hath begun a good work in you, will [continue to] perform it until the day of Jesus Christ" (Phil. 1:6). I could multiply verses like these and say, "Well, they contradict." No, they don't contradict!

One set of verses is talking about the gift of God that gives to us eternal life, and other verses deal with the manifestation of this salvation. Some people's lives seem to have little fruit. Yet may I remind you that God keeps the books, and the computers of heaven never miss a thing.

Some little lady out here in the country you would look at and say, "Well, she is fruitless." She may be more fruitful than you could ever know. She may have touched a life that's been everything. Do you know the man who touched the life of D. L. Moody? He sold Moody a pair of shoes that day. What about him? His life could have been pretty barren. But think of this— he will be clipping coupons in all eternity on D. L. Moody. Just think of it! He touched the life of one man.

So we have to be careful in our judgment. You say, "Pastor, you believe a certain way because this is the way you were taught." No, this is what the Word of God says, and I have to be very honest with the Word of God. I have to take the passages that teach us that we are safe in His hands and ask, "Now what do these passages teach?"

I think that you will find that one has to do with "root" and the other with "fruit." No one would have ever believed that when they looked in at Sodom and saw Lot in the mayor's office, that he was a saved man. But he was. God said, "I can't destroy this city until I get him out, because he belongs to Me." And Lot had not been living for God at all. It is an Old Testament picture of what God does for a believer.

199. Old Testament Salvation

What is the role of the Holy Spirit in Old Testament salvation?

Dr. Sugden: Abraham was saved by faith. All the folk in the Old Testament were saved by faith, and they were saved by faith in the One who *was* coming. We are saved by faith in the One who *has* come, so the cross becomes the central position in the program and in the economy of God. Old Testament saints were saved just like we are saved. They were saved by faith.

I was at an ordination not long ago, and someone asked the candidate for ordination, "How were the Old Testament saints saved?" He said, "They were saved by keeping the law." Do you know what? Not one person said a word. They all said, "Now, isn't that lovely," and they voted to ordain him.

Old Testament saints were NOT saved by keeping the law. They were saved by looking forward to the Messiah who was going to come. They believed in Him, looking forward by faith as we now look back by faith to Him.

The Holy Spirit's ministry in the Old Testament was vastly different from what it is today. He came upon men to empower them and use them. On *no occasion* did He come to indwell them. In the New Testament, He comes to indwell us and to live in us when we are saved. That is the difference.

Gideon was filled with the Spirit. He blew a trumpet. A number of functions operate in the Holy Spirit's work in the Old Testament, but His work was different than it is at the present time.

Mrs. Sugden: They were saved by faith in their sacrifices, which were types and pictures of the sacrifice of the Lamb of God.

Dr. Sugden: When they brought their sacrifices, they were saying, "We see Jesus."

200. Predestination

The Bible says that "God is not willing that any should perish," and that "Christ died for all men" (2 Peter 3:9; 2 Cor. 5:15). It also says in several places that we are chosen in Him. I have heard it preached that God has chosen specific people to be saved. This seems to indicate that others are left out by God. I cannot fathom our God not giving all men the chance to receive or reject Him. Can you clarify this?

Dr. Sugden: I think God chooses groups. He chose Israel as a nation. They were a chosen nation. I think the church is a chosen body. If we are in the church, we are chosen because the church is a chosen body. It is an elected body, as Israel was an elected nation. I think if you leave it there you will always be safe. You can't get away from the Bible, which teaches that

Christ died for all and that whosoever will may come. It is constantly saying, "whosoever."

It does not say, "whosoever, if you are elect." You don't know if they are elect, anyway. And having said this, may I suggest to you that election in the Word of God always has to do with privilege. Predestination has to do with privilege. We are predestined to be conformed; we are predestined for blessing. It never says we were predestined for hell.

I have studied this for fifty years. I have read everything there is on the subject. The greatest book on it is the Bible itself. Sometime you need to sit down and read through the gospel of John and mark the word "world." Let me give you one.

Here is John the Baptist, and he is along the river Jordan. Suddenly Jesus comes down. He lifts his hand and points and says: "Behold the Lamb of God, which taketh away the sin of the *world* (John 1:29). And it does not say "the world of the elect!"

201. Salvation and Inerrancy of Scripture

Can a person be truly born again and have eternal life even if he does not believe in the literal inerrant Word of God?

Mrs. Sugden: I'm so glad we are not the judge. We leave that up to God.

Dr. Sugden: Yes, we will leave that with God. However, let us be honest. If you believe in the Lord Jesus, you have to believe the Bible.

I was at a pastors' conference. One of the liberal men stood up and told me to be quiet about the Bible being the Word of God. He said that the Bible is dividing us. Then he said, "Why don't you just be honest and tell people about Jesus? Skip talking about the Bible."

I asked him, "Will you please explain to me where would I get my information about Jesus?"

How would you find out about the Lord Jesus if you did not have the Word of God? You would not know about His virgin birth, His life, nor His death. You would not know about His resurrection, His ascension, and that He is now seated at the right hand of God if it were not for the Word of God.

They are tied together. So I would say that a person would have to believe in the authority of the Word of God if he is going to believe and receive Jesus as His Savior.

202. Saved in Childbearing

Please explain 1 Timothy 2:15.

Dr. Sugden: First let us look at the verses of context: "For Adam was first formed, then Eve. And Adam was not deceived, but the women being deceived was in the transgression. Notwithstanding she shall be saved in childbearing, if they continue in faith and charity and holiness with sobriety" (1 Tim. 2:13-15).

After reading everything I possibly could on this (and you may disagree with me), I think this is a reference to the birth of the Messiah. The salvation that came to us, not only to women but to the whole world, came because Mary gave birth to Jesus.

203. Second Chance of Salvation

Will those who have heard the gospel and rejected it have a chance to accept the Lord in the tribulation?

Dr. Sugden: Let me read from 2 Thessalonians 2, beginning at verse 9: "Even him, whose coming is after the working of Satan with all power and signs and lying wonders, and with all deceivableness . . ." (2 Thess. 2:9, 10).

Paul is talking about someone who is going to appear on this earth. He has not yet appeared. Antichrist has not been here. But he will come, and he will practice deception.

Now verse 11: "And for this cause God shall send them strong delusion, that they should believe the lie . . ."

It is a lie, but it is *the* lie, "that they all might be damned who believed not the truth" (2 Thess. 2:12).

Suppose the Lord should come and the Antichrist should appear. You say, "Pastor, I don't believe in any anyway, so why bother." But let me say that I do. Supposing the Lord should come and the Antichrist should appear with all deceivableness—that is what he is going to do. The Book of Revelation is crowded with it. He said that those who had an opportunity will not be given another chance. That's what it says. They will believe the lie.

204. Salvation During the Tribulation

Is it possible to be saved during the tribulation?

Dr. Sugden: Yes, we do know that there will be salvation. The evidence is in the Book of Revelation. During the time of the tribulation recorded in chapters 6 through 19, you have the 144,000. Now these 144,000 are not the Jehovah's Witnesses cult. They claim that they are the Jehovah's Witnesses of that period, but I believe the Bible is talking about Jews.

In that tribulation period, God does a special work with the twelve tribes. Out of each tribe there are twelve thousand taken, until there are 144,000. These 144,000 are going to be God's messengers during the tribulation period. If the apostle Paul is an example of what one Jewish man will do, just think of what will happen when you have 144,000 like the apostle Paul!

In Revelation 7, after the 144,000 are taken (and they apparently go out into the world to witness), you have that remarkable statement: "After this I behold, and, lo, a great multitude, which no man could number, of all nations, and kindreds and people, and tongues. . ." (Rev. 7:9).

What happened? I think these 144,000 had taken 747's and little Cessnas and they had flown. They moved down the skyways and the roadways of the world and heralded the message wherever they were. Those who had never heard, now believed.

205. Universal Salvation

If God is not willing that any should perish, according to 2 Peter 3:9, then is it not God's will that all be saved? If we as Christians pray and ask in Jesus' name for someone to be saved, is it possible for this one to die unsaved? What role does the will of the unsaved one have in this case?

Mrs. Sugden: It has everything to do with it.

Dr. Sugden: We believe, and this is part of the great structure of our orthodox faith and of biblical Christianity, that the atonement of Jesus Christ and the work of the cross was sufficient for all men. It is operative and sufficient in those who believe.

At one time I just saturated my soul on one word in the gospel of John—the word "world." I know all the explanations and all the interpretations, but I do not think you can take the world and make it skinny. You can't say that God meant half of the world, or a third of the world, or a quarter of the world. I believe that God really loved the whole world of men. He gave His Son, and there is a going forth of the gospel message that we designate for "whosoever will may come."

I believe that those who are dealt with by the Spirit of God are moved to come to receive the Lord Jesus as their Savior.

The invitation is universal, and it is sufficient for everyone that responds. Those who come are saved by simple faith in Jesus Christ.

Mrs. Sugden: God doesn't force Himself on us. Your will has to be broken and your heart opened to believe in Christ.

16
SIN AND FORGIVENESS

206. Confession of Sin

Roman Catholics confess their sins to a priest, believing that God forgives them because of their sincere, humble confession. Is this similar to what we're exhorted to do in 1 John 1:9? If, however, they are not really born again, even though they walk in the light they have, what is the best way to effectively witness to a Roman Catholic?

Dr. Sugden: Funny things happen to me. I had a funeral the other day, and we had a limousine. The pallbearers were in the back seat, six of them. I did not know the deceased, but I knew his family. I didn't realize that many of his friends, in fact the six men in the car, were Roman Catholic.

They were very gracious and kind to me, and I listened to their conversation. They talked about the church. One of them said, "Do you go to confession any more?" Another answered, "Yes, what about you?" One of them said, "I skip it."

As they talked about confession, one of them asked the one who said he went, "Why do you go? You know he can't forgive your sins."

The answer was amazing! "I know he can't forgive my sins, but it certainly gets a load off my chest."

Now stop and think about that! This man was saying something: "The very fact that I can sit down and say what's inside of me, and get it out where I can see it, is doing me good."

Now that view is not Christian. God made us a promise. Many Christians do not know what to do when they stumble. They just go on hurting. Many say to me, "Yes, I was saved."

But what happened? They tell me what they did to fall. Maybe it was something like a mountain, or maybe it was a pebble. But they sinned, and they found themselves estranged and separated from God.

When you make a mistake as a child, your greatest need at that moment is your parent. When you sin, the greatest need you have is to be with God. Don't allow things to accumulate. Learn early in life to confess immediately to Him. Set the records straight. "If we confess our sins, He is faithful and just to forgive us our sins, and to cleanse us from all unrighteousness" (1 John 1:9).

You say, "Pastor, how many times can we go back and confess?" I don't know the times. But I do know that when Peter asked that question, he said, "How oft shall my brother sin against me, and I forgive him? till seven times?" (Matt. 18:20). But note the reply: "Jesus said unto him, I say not unto thee, until seven times: but until seventy times seven" (Matt. 18:22).

This is the ultimate. God is in the business of forgiving and restoring. Perhaps you are uncomfortable in your heart. How do you find relief? Confess, and He forgives.

Then, I think the best way to deal with Roman Catholics is to be their friend. They need to know 1 Timothy 2:5, and you can share it with them: "For there is one God, and one mediator between God and men, the man Christ Jesus."

207. Discipline

Please explain the meaning of Hebrews 12:9, which reads: "Furthermore we have had fathers of our flesh which corrected us, and we gave them reverence: shall we not much rather be in subjection to the Father of spirits, and live?"

Dr. Sugden: This refers to the discipline of God. In our natural family a father corrects his children. What if a Christian sins? God corrects him. He does just what an earthly father does.

My father did that, and I'm glad he did. Some of the greatest things he ever did for me were the good "shoelacings" he gave me. I didn't appreciate it then, but I learned obedience and subjection to him.

When God deals with us, He does the same thing. The 12th chapter of Hebrews deals with the disciplinary actions of God. A Christian sins. He does that which is wrong. God says, "All right, I'll have to correct you." So He corrects you.

He says, "As you have been subject to earthly fathers, be subject to your Heavenly Father." Say to Him, "Thank you, Lord; thank You for what You are doing for me today. You are helping me."

208. Forgiveness

Please give the passage or verse that tells us to forgive when we have been wronged, even when we haven't been asked to forgive.

Dr. Sugden: I went through the entire New Testament, especially the gospels, on that aspect of forgiveness. I don't think you can find anywhere that you are to forgive people without their asking. How do you know they are angry? How do you know they are disturbed, if they haven't talked with you? You have to be aware of it before you can forgive.

When we are aware that things have gone wrong, then we have something we can do. Look at Matthew 18. There is not a word in this chapter about forgiveness. But you realize that when the disciples reacted to this, they understood that here was something that needed to be forgiven and set right, because Peter said so. "Moreover if thy brother shall trespass against thee, go and tell him his fault between thee and him alone. . ." (Matt. 18:15).

Suppose you have a problem with a brother. What are you to do? Let it fester? Let it become nasty? Talk about it to the whole church and get everybody upset? No!

If a brother has wronged you, you are go to to him. It doesn't even say to go to the pastor, or your friends, or get on the telephone. Don't make it public. We would save about 90 percent of the church's problems if we'd just start to practice this principle.

So, if a brother sins or trespasses against you, tell him his fault between you and him alone. Don't go to him and say, "Listen here, I've got to have a word with you, you louse. You know that I was right."

No, don't go that way. Go and say, "You know, I'm so glad that God is our Father. We belong to Him, and you're my brother, and it isn't right for us to go on this way."

This is the way you do it. You can shake a big stick and create a fuss; or you can set things right in a Christian way. The Christian way is to go to him, and tell him his fault between you and him alone. Then, "if he shall hear thee, thou hast gained thy brother" (Matt. 18:15). You don't lose anything. You gain a brother. A fellow said, "But I'll lose face if I do that."

Now notice what it says: "But if he will not hear thee. . . (Matt. 18:16). Suppose you go to him and he says, "No sir, I don't have any time for you." What do you do? I take one or two with me, and we go to him. We attempt to settle the problem. If that doesn't work, then it is to be brought before the board of the church. The men that are on the board represent the church. That is why we have boards.

You say, "I don't see anything about forgiveness in this passage." Look at verse 21: "Then came Peter to Him, and said, Lord, how oft shall my brother sin against me, and I forgive him?" They understood that this was a matter of forgiveness between people. Peter was right there on the spot, and he said, "How many times can my brother come to me and sin against me? till seven times?" And poor Peter hit the deck! The Lord answered: "I say not unto thee, Until seven times: but, Until seventy times seven" (Matt. 18:22).

Do you sense something of the magnitude of the forgiveness of God in this? He expects me to forgive 490 times! So I gather that in every situation, regardless of how you want to construct it, as believers we are to practice the noble art, not of self-defense, but the noble art of forgiveness.

Do you know how I am to forgive? In Ephesians 4:32, Paul told me I am to forgive as Christ forgave me. If we did, it could make some tremendous changes in our local churches. When we begin to set things right, great things happen, and blessings come.

209. Iniquity and Transgression

What is the difference between iniquity, transgression, and sin?

Dr. Sugden: When the children of Israel met on the day of Atonement (Lev. 15), they met so that the sacrifice of that day might put away iniquity, transgression, and sin. When the high priest stood and confessed over the goat's head all of Israel's iniquities, transgressions, and sins, it was like "clearing the decks." It covered everything that man had done which was contrary to God. Now look at it in Psalm 32: "Blessed is he whose transgression is forgiven, whose sin is covered. Blessed is the man unto whom the Lord imputeth not iniquity..." (Psalm 32:1, 2).

Note: "transgression" means "to walk across." It literally means to rebel against. So here is somebody who had a rebellious spirit. What has God done? He has forgiven his transgression.

The word "sin" used here is the Hebrew word meaning, "to miss the mark." You put up a target, and you miss the mark; you have a goal and you never make it. You miss the mark. You wanted to be like this, but you failed along the way. So your transgression is forgiven; your sin is covered.

The word "iniquity" is a great word because it has to do with the bias. It means "to be bent." The most perfect thing you have as an example is lawn bowling. You have a ball with a weight on one side, and you can curve it either way.

Man is by nature weighted away from God. He is naturally involved with iniquity, because he has a built-in bias. It is natural for man to go away from God. So what does God do? He takes care of our transgressions, our rebellious natures. He takes care of the failures of our lives, and He takes care of that iniquity that bends us away from God. That's what He does. "Iniquity" is a great word.

When that happens, we should be happy. We used to sing a little chorus that said, "Oh, say but I'm glad, I'm glad." Well, you can be, because this Psalm was fulfilled. Leviticus 15 was also fulfilled that day when Christ died and took our transgressions, our sins, and our iniquities. He settled it forever.

210. Restoration of a Backslider

How do you restore Christians who have been backslidden for many years? How do you discern whether they are really Christians? Some claim to be, yet show no hunger for God or His Word.

Dr. Sugden: We are encouraged in Galatians 6:1 "to restore such an one." We read: "Brethren, if a man be overtaken in a fault, ye which are spiritual, restore such an one in the spirit of meekness; considering thyself, lest thou also be tempted."

I believe, first of all, that we will never restore anyone until he has confidence in us. In this area we have to have a very low estimate of ourselves. We do not go to the fallen one and say, "I wish you were like I am." I think we go to him with love and compassion, and we talk to him.

Be a friend to him first. Know something about him. Maybe you already do, but you may know the wrong thing. Find out about his experience. It is not difficult to ask him about his relationship with the Lord. Say, "I've been watching you, and you're saved, aren't you?"

Put it positively, or immediately you have a negative and he is turned off. When I have said, "You're a Christian, aren't you?" I have found out people will say, "Yes, I am, but I'm not living like one."

"Oh, you're not?" I have had the response over and over again.

The greatest work we need to be involved in, in the local church, is with people who once began with God, but have lost out along the way. They feel shunned. They are hurt. Above all, no one cares. Restoration is a godly work. Learn to practice it. Do it with kindness, tenderness, and compassion.

If there is no response, you don't say, "Well, he did not respond to me. I will not go back again." Sometimes you go again and again and again. This could be the great work of your life, if you begin to do it now.

211. Sins of the Flesh

I have been captive for years with a lust, but have gained victory. However, I still experience times when I am deeply attracted to the old way. How can I get rid of this weakness?

Dr. Sugden: It is not easy. During a pastors' conference, a young pastor came to me and asked if he could talk. We found a quiet place, and he told me about his life.

During his war years he lived a wild life such as you could not believe. I gasped! I couldn't believe it. He said, "I'm now a pastor, preaching and teaching the Word of God. I love my people, and I do all the things a pastor should do."

Then he said, "There are days when I just have to run and pray, and ask the Lord to wipe my mind clean. I remember all those nights, a new woman every night of my life, and all the things that went on."

He said, "There are days when it just drives me up the wall. So what would you do?"

I said, "Exactly what you are doing. Ask God to cleanse your mind. God will do it. He is the business of doing it."

He does take care of the mind. His promises are, "Thou wilt keep him in perfect peace whose mind is stayed on Thee" (Isa. 26:3); and "The peace of God which passeth all understanding, shall keep [guard] your heart and mind" (Phil. 4:7). The word "keep" is "guard." It is a military word. They put a guard around the camp. Paul looked out and said, "There they are." That's what God does for me. He puts a guard around me. So we have to bring our thoughts into subjection. That's not easy to do, but God can do it.

212. Sin Unto Death

Please explain 1 John 5:16, 17 concerning the sin unto death and the sin not unto death.

Dr. Sugden: Look at the passage: "If any man see his brother sin a sin which is not unto death, he shall ask, and He shall give him life for them that sin not unto death. There is a sin unto death: I do not say that he shall pray for it. All unrighteousness is sin: and there is a sin not unto death . . ."

I think that a sin that is *not* unto death is a sin that God will forgive and cleanse and restore. We all probably do things in our lives that are displeasing to God. But God doesn't kill us. He doesn't take away our lives.

Now, you have to be careful because you can take some scripture verses and make them "clubs." It was my misfortune, when I was a kid, to have a pastor who delighted in grabbing scriptural clubs and assaulting the saints. This is one of the dangers. He used to say, "Well, that man did something to me, and do you see what's happened to him? We buried him last week."

I've discovered that if you live long enough, most of your enemies will die ahead of you. So you can't take the Scriptures and prove anything by that. But I've seen men do it. They're doing it today. They say, "Well, did you see what happened to him? He opposed me, and he died, didn't he?"

That doesn't mean anything. Everyone has an appointed time to die. But the Word of God teaches that it is possible for a Christian to go on in his course of rebellion, with wickedness in his heart, and God will deal with him and remove him by death. But I don't get up in the pulpit and use this as a club. We'd better leave that with God. It is always better in God's hands than in ours.

You say, "Pastor, where is that?" Let's turn to it in 1 Corinthians 11:26. I'm speaking now about what my pastor used to do, because I was a Christian for a long time before I ever took the Lord's supper. It became a terrifying experience to me. He used to terrify the people at the Lord's table.

"For as often as he eat this bread, and drink this cup, ye do show the Lord's death till he come."

That word "show" is the word for "communicate." Do you know that when we have the Lord's table, we communicate? People look on and say, "Isn't that wonderful? What's happening?'' It is apparent that there were unbelievers in the service in Corinth when they had the Lord's table.

Some of the greatest moments of our lives have taken place around the Lord's table. Christians set things right with themselves, right where they sit. I remember a dear little Scottish family who came and sat down three seats from the front. I had never seen them in church before. When they came to my door after the service was over, I said, ''You are new here today.'' They said, ''How did you know?''

I said, ''You haven't been here before. That's why you are new here.''

They were the loveliest couple. Then she turned to her husband, and asked him if he was going to talk to me now or later. He said, ''What do you mean?'' She reminded him of what they had said during the Lord's table during the service. Then they told me they were believers, but they hadn't been in church for a long time. They said, ''We've been so far away, but this morning when you talked at the Lord's table, God spoke to us.''

She had reached over and touched her husband's hand and said to him, ''Don't you think it's about time that we asked God to forgive us and get restored?'' He said, ''Yes, I do,''and at the Lord's table they were restored into fellowship.

''Wherefore whosoever shall eat this bread, and drink this cup of the Lord, unworthily. . .'' (1 Cor. 11:27).

The word ''unworthily'' used to frighten me. My pastor would dwell on the ''unworthily.'' If you have been unworthy, what is going to happen to you? Look at verse 30: ''For this cause many are weak and sickly among you, and many sleep [have died]. . .'' (1 Cor. 11:30).

That, I think, goes with what we read in 1 John 5. It is probably the sin unto death. Again, the Bible is silent about what this sin is, as only Paul says, ''in an unworthy manner, not discerning the Lord's body.''

This passage has to be dealt with, but there are lots of sins we commit that are not unto death. You ask, ''Do you think that Christians sin?'' I know some that do. We sin in many ways—thoughts and words and deeds. ''If we say we have not sinned, we deceive ourselves,and the truth is not in us. If we confess our sins, He is faithful and just to forgive us our sins, and to cleanse us from all righteousness'' (1 John 1:8, 9). There is a sin unto death. I think we'd best leave it in God's hands.

213. Unpardonable Sin

What is the unpardonable sin? Does it relate to the sin unto death?

Dr. Sugden: The sin unto death has nothing to do with the unpardonable sin. The unpardonable sin was a specific sin that took place when the Lord Jesus was on earth. I do not believe that it can be committed today.

Dr. Lewis Sperry Chafer, at one time president of the Dallas Theological Seminary, said that it is impossible to have the grace of God preached and have unpardonable sin.

The unforgiven sin is a different matter. The unforgiven sin is the sin of unbelief. If a person goes on in life and does not believe in Jesus Christ, that is an unforgiven sin. For that sin they shut themselves off from God. Sad to say, hell is their destiny.

Look at Mark 3:22. "And the scribes which came down from Jerusalem said . . ." Now listen, here are the Jewish scribes, the men who wrote the law of God. Speaking of Jesus, they said, "He hath Beelzebub, and by the prince of the devils casteth He out devils."

Here was the Lord Jesus, right in their midst. What was He doing? He was performing miracles. The people acknowledged Him as God, as the Son of God. These scribes came down and said, "This is the devil. He does his power by the devil." That's what they said of the Lord Jesus.

"And He called them unto Him, and said unto them in parables, How can Satan cast out Satan?" (Mark 3:32).

Satan doesn't go around kicking himself out.

"And if a kingdom be divided against itself, that kingdom cannot stand. And if a house be divided against itself, that house cannot stand. And if Satan rise up against himself, and be divided, he cannot stand, but hath an end" (Mark 3:24-26).

Jesus is saying that if Satan is working against himself, that's something new to Me. Satan is for himself.

"No man can enter into a strong man's house, and spoil his goods, except he will first bind the strong man; and then he will spoil his house.

Verily I say unto you [now, here is the crux of it], All sins shall be forgiven unto the sons of men, and blasphemies wherewithsoever they shall blaspheme:

But he that shall blaspheme against the Holy Spirit hath never forgiveness, but is in danger of eternal damnation" (Mark 3:28, 29).

Then He told what the sin is: "Because they said, He hath an unclean spirit" (Mark 3:30). It is amazing that this happened in that day when Jesus was there, performing miracles. They could see Him, they could hear Him, they could look on Him. He said, "You will have no forgiveness for this sin; they had called Him a devil."

214. Willful Sin

Hebrews 6:4-9 and Hebrews 10:26 are considered difficult passages. Could you please comment on them?

Dr. Sugden: When you read in the epistle of Hebrews that there is no more sacrifice for sin, you say, "That is an awesome thing, isn't it?"

Yes, it is. But it becomes clear when you realize that if I were a Hebrew, I would bring my sacrifice to God this morning. Then when I did wrong, I would bring another sacrifice, and another, every morning.

But the Hebrews writer in the New Testament says there is no other sacrifice but Jesus. That's finality, isn't it? You don't do now what you did in Old Testament days. You don't bring another sacrifice. There is one sacrifice, so it is a contrast between the many and the one.

He says that you used to bring a sacrifice for sin, but now there is no more sacrifice for sin. That sacrifice and settlement of sin has been forever made. You don't need to bring one.

A fellow came to an evangelist friend of mine and said, "What can I do for my salvation?"

He said, "You are too late."

He asked, "How late am I?"

He said, "Nineteen hundred years too late." Everything that had to be done, has been done.

Now look at Hebrews 10:26: "For if we sin wilfully after that we have received the knowledge of the truth, there remaineth no more sacrifice for sins."

Of course, there isn't. There is no more sacrifice for sin. That sacrifice for sin was made. They could keep bringing and bringing and bringing, but God says you don't do that any more. You can't bring another sacrifice for sin, because the sacrifice for sin has been made.

Now note: "But a certain fearful looking for of judgment and fiery indignation, which shall devour the adversaries" (Hebrews 10:27). He is talking about the Old Testament, when they brought sacrifices. Isn't it something that it doesn't say, "He that broke Moses' law?" It doesn't say that. It says: "He that despised Moses' law . . ." (Hebrews 10:28).

If you despise the law, or if you despise the offering God has made for sin, there is no hope. You cannot despise Jesus and be saved. So the author of Hebrews is talking about salvation, and about despising the Lord Jesus.

17
SPIRIT BEINGS

215. Ministry of Angels

Is the ministry of angels important in this present age?

Dr. Sugden: Angels are a significant study in the Scriptures. Many volumes are written on angels. Sometime when you are in a theological library and have an hour, get a book on angels and scan it. It is a wonderful study.

The greatest verse on angels is the last verse of Hebrews 1. The chapter begins, "God, who at sundry times and in divers manners spake. . . ." (Hebrews 1:1).

God spoke all through the Old Testament in different ways. He was moving, moving, moving. And then He moved to finality, and look what He did. He spoke by His son. He is not going to speak any more. He spoke by His son.

And then He brings in angels (v. 4). Who are the angels? He tells all about the angels. Then He comes to this magnificent verse. I'm giving you Weymouth's translation, which is just super! "Are not all angels spirits that serve Him—whom He sends out to render service for the benefit of those who, before long, will inherit salvation?" (Hebrews 1:14). Who are the angels? They are God's servants who are, hour by hour, being dispatched unto us, we are the heirs of salvation. I never read that verse but what I think about our airport.

Our airport in Lansing is skinny; it is not a big airport like Toronto. But it has airplanes and a big tower. I have been up in that tower. The men sit up there and have screens all around them. Planes are coming in and planes are leaving. The controller says, "Plane number 422," and he directs.

As I sat up there, I said, "That's Hebrews 1:14." Isn't it? Here is God, and He says, "Angel number 7, take care of Mrs. Sugden this morning. Angel number 12, take care of the family this morning."

He directs the angels. They are God's ministering servants who are being dispatched to us. We are not only in good hands, but He has angels for us. It is great to know about the angels, God's servants who minister to us.

216. Satan's Power

Can Satan read our minds? Can he put evil thoughts in our minds?

Mrs. Sugden: He certainly can put evil thoughts in our minds. That's for sure.

Dr. Sugden: When we ask this question, we put it in a theological context. We ask, "Is Satan omniscient?"

My answer to that is, "He is NOT omniscient." I do not believe that Satan is omniscient as God is omniscient. I doubt that Satan knows your thoughts. God knows, but He has never said that Satan knows.

But Satan can put evil thoughts in our minds. How does he do this? Today is probably the most difficult day in which to live, because we have all kinds of contrivances for evil thoughts around us.

For instance, have you ever considered how many evil thoughts come galloping into our living rooms like frightened horses when some TV show is on? Right now we are doing studies in the United States on what is happening to the children because of TV.

I think we will never discover the devastation that has come through TV in our homes. For some children, television is their entertainment. They don't have babysitters. They have TV. They come home from school and get down on the floor with potato chips and coke. They have all this junk food and then watch the TV. They are TV children, and it is a disastrous thing.

Satan comes into our minds through what we read and what we see. Satan captures our minds in many ways. Just think of what he is doing with pornographic material in our world today.

So all this evil comes into our minds. But the Lord has to guard our minds. He really has and I think He will continue to do so. He said: "Thou wilt keep him in perfect peace, whose mind is stayed on Thee: because he trusteth in Thee" (Isaiah 26:3).

217. Spiritism

My brother was killed in an accident several years ago. My aunt, a minister of the spiritualist church, claims to be able to contact this brother. She says she has tape recordings of him.

Who exactly is she contacting? Could it really be my brother?
Did the witch of Endor really contact Samuel at Saul's wishes?
If so, how could this be?

Dr. Sugden: That is spiritism, pure and simple—pure and simple fakery.

Mrs. Sugden: Then who is she contacting?

Dr. Sugden: If she is in contact with anyone, it is certainly not God. It is not an angel. It must be satanic.

Mrs. Sugden: It is not the brother.

Dr. Sugden: No, it is not the brother. The Bible says in Luke 16:26 that "there is a great gulf fixed." One man is here, and one is in the other world. It says they do not pass over. How can you do anything with that?

Mrs. Sugden: She does not say whether the brother was saved or not. Does that make a difference?

Dr. Sugden: I don't think so.

Now let us take the witch of Endor in 1 Samuel 28. Here she was, sitting in her little tent, wrapped up in her loveliness, having on all the dangles in her ears. She was sitting there as this witch. Saul comes along and says, "I would like you to call up a man."

God had left Saul. He had sinned away his days so badly that God was not communicating with him. Saul was trying to grasp at something. He had already made an edict to destroy all the witches; everyone who was trying to do that kind of work.

Witches were forbidden, and they were to be destroyed. So Saul thought he had gotten along quite well. But someone told him, "There is one left. You have missed her. She is down there, and she does a good job. Go down and see her."

So Saul went down and said, "I want this man"(v. 8). But when Samuel appeared, the witch was dumbfounded. She had never had this happen to her before in her life. It had all been fakery. But God allowed Samuel to come back to say one last word to Saul, who had so defeated the purpose of God.

Mrs. Sugden: What body did Samuel have?

Dr. Sugden: Just like he had on earth, which is another proof of how we are going to look in heaven. He even had on the same clothes.

Mrs. Sugden: Was it an illusion?

Dr. Sugden: No, I think he really came. I have read everything I could on this. I think the evidence is that he came. He was so real that Saul was shocked, and the witch was shocked. Then Samuel told Saul what was going to happen to him, which is an evidence that it was real.

18
WITNESSING

218. Dealing With Athiests

How do you deal with an athiest?

Dr. Sugden: Athiests are a strange crowd. I have never met a man who was really an athiest. I have met folk who said they were. The only man I ever met who was almost an athiest stood in our little community and cursed God. He talked about God. He blasphemed God. Then suddenly, when the death rattle came, he changed his mind.

I think you witness to an athiest graciously and kindly. If he has a problem about belief in God, quietly say to him, "Please explain everything you see. You have to have an explanation. How do you explain this?

Some of my most exciting experiences are in hospitals. Someone calls and says, "Pastor Sugden, we have an uncle in the hospital who is an athiest. You would enjoy going to see him, wouldn't you?"

Oh, yes, I would. So I go, and I expect to meet some cursing, damning old man. One day I walked through the door and there sat a man on the edge of the bed. I said, "You wouldn't know who I am, but I am Pastor Sugden."

Would you believe it? The man began to cry. He said, "Why are you here?"

I said, "Because somebody thought of you. They told me that if I came to see you, I'd find a lovely man."

He said, "Interesting."

I talked with him, and he was saved. Just be patient, but sow seeds. I ask them to tell me how they explain creation. I say, "How do you explain *you?* How do you explain the fact that while you talk to me about not believing in God, you know deep down in your heart that there is one?" Because he does.

Every man is made with that capacity. He tries to squeeze it out, but he isn't able to do so. The very fact that he is unable to squeeze it out is demonstrated in the fact that he fights against God.

You don't fight against people that don't exist, do you? Imagine a boxer fighting against somebody who isn't there.

Think of Madelyn Murray O'Hair saying, "There is no God," and later her son is saved. He is now talking about the wonder of God.

Mrs. Sugden: I think you have to witness outside of the Bible, because they don't believe the Bible. Like you said, behind everything that has been created there must be a Maker. However, I think it is good to give a verse of Scripture, because it is amazing what the Word does.

Dr. Sugden: Give them a short verse.

219. Dealing With Jehovah's Witness

For the past four months I have been working with a Jehovah's Witness. They disagree with most, if not all, of our Christian doctrine, in particular the trinity. I have shown him all the passages from the Bible that my pastor and I found to substantiate the trinity, but he was able to turn them around.

Dr. Sugden: They are gifted in turning things around. When you wrestle with cults, you wrestle with the impossible. Their minds are like concrete, mixed and set. It is hard to do anything with somebody who is mixed up and permanently set in it.

You can confront them with the truth. You ask if they are ever rescued. We have former Jehovah's Witnesses in our house of God who have been saved, but there are not many.

The same thing is true with the Mormons. I think the Mormons are the most abominable cult. They are reproducing. They go out two by two, but they make the folk they reach worse than they were before they were reached.

Mrs. Sugden: Give to the Mormon the Book of Colossians. I had a man in my Sunday school class who came out of Jehovah's Witnesses, and it was Colossians that helped him see the truth.

Dr. Sugden: First of all, let's look at 2 Corinthians 13, beginning at verse 11:

> ". . . Be perfect, be of good comfort, be of one mind, live in peace; and the God of love and peace shall be with you.
> Greet one another with an holy kiss. All the saints salute you. The grace of the Lord Jesus Christ, and the love of God, and the communion of the Holy Ghost be with you all. Amen" (2 Cor. 13:11-14).

Now what does that say? It says that there is a God who is the

Father; there is the Lord Jesus Christ; and there is a Holy Spirit. It is not called "trinity," but when you have three like this, we call it trinity. That is what the Bible teaches.

The best proof (one they can't wiggle out of) is found in this passage: "And Jesus, when He was baptized, went up straightway out of the water: and, lo, the heavens were opened unto Him, and He saw the Spirit of God descending like a dove, and lighting upon Him: And lo a voice from heaven, saying, This is My beloved Son, in whom I am well pleased" (Matthew 3:16, 17).

The Son obeys, the Spirit descends, and the Father speaks. If I were to see the Lord Jesus baptized, and look up and see the Holy Spirit come in the form of a dove upon Him, and hear a voice from God speak, I would be inclined to believe that there was God the Father, God the Son, and God the Holy Spirit.

No one who will be honest in the exegesis of the Word of God could say, "Well, that is not what it means." What does it mean then, if it doesn't mean that the Son of God was baptized and the Spirit of God descended and God the Father spoke?

The greatest thing to turn them off is to say, "Oh, you believe in the kingdom, don't you?" I asked two of them this one day, and they said, "Oh, yes."

Then I said, "I'm always interested in you folk because you are a part of the kingdom, aren't you?"

They said, "Yes, we are."

I said, "Well, that's fine; then I suppose you are born again, aren't you?" That turns them off. They said, "No, we don't believe in that."

I said, "All right, but the Bible says, '. . . except a man be born again, he cannot see the kingdom of God' (John 3:3)."

And do you know what? They left.

220. Witnessing to the Bereaved

How do you comfort and lead to the Lord, an unsaved woman whose unsaved husband just died? To introduce her to the Lord would be to tell her of eternity in heaven with Christ for herself. But her husband's eternity is in hell.

Dr. Sugden: I think that if you are to be a purveyor of comfort, you will have to put the difficult problems of your task aside. Don't discuss her husband's situation. Deal with her about comfort. Talk about the comfort that she will need now and in the tomorrows.

I live with death and sorrow every day. My responsibility is to communicate the Word of God and the promises of God in such a way that those who are not saved will be saved; and that those who are saved will be comforted and encouraged.

I would tell this lady about what the Lord Jesus could do for her in the immediate now and in her tomorrows. Tell her she needs strength and help, and that the Lord can give it to her. Then, as she comes to know and enjoy personally the Lord Jesus, the other problem will be minimal and will in a large measure be dissipated.

I am amazed at how many of my men I have buried in thirty years of ministry in our house of God. We have probably a hundred women in our church whose husbands are dead. They seem to get along quite well. They have their little groups of friends, and they love each other, care for each other, and support each other. I am always encouraged by this, because I see what the Lord can do in the personal life of an individual.

And there is a sense in which the Lord causes us to forget: to forget our sorrows and our hurts. This saves us from becoming morbid. It really does. So God has a way of filling in and filling full and filling to overflowing our lives, so that we are able to go on and live triumphantly.

Death is not an easy thing to face. But God, who is the giver of life and the giver of compassion and comfort, has a wonderful way of caring for us. We will face the impossible, and walk around our Jerichos' and the walls will fall flat before us.

221. Witnessing to Unsaved Loved Ones

I have just become a Christian. Now I must go home to my family. They are not Christians, and I am concerned about how they will react. What can I expect?

Dr. Sugden: I have a special interest in this young man, because last week I was privileged to lead him to Christ. I think if I were this young man, when I arrived home I would tell them what happened at the proper time. I would probably do it at mealtime, because everybody is happy when they're eating.

You know what I would say? I'd say, "Because I have become a Christian, I have a new love and a new appreciation for you that I never had before."

Isn't it great that when you become a part of God's family, you are given an increased love and affection for your own family? I would explain to them that now, because I am a

Christian, I hold them in esteem and I love them as I have never loved them before. "Isn't it wonderful, Dad and Mom, that I'm going to be able to pray for you that God will help you?"

I don't think any family could ever look down and say, "Oh, shut up." I don't think so, because here is somebody saying, "I love you more than I've ever loved you before, because I'm a part of God's family."

That's the way salvation is. Our human love is almost a divine love when we know the Lord.

19
WOMEN

222. Duty of Wives

Will you please comment on 1 Peter 3:1-7 concerning the gentle, quiet spirit of a woman? And on the husband's relationship to his wife, as given in verse 7?

"Likewise, ye wives, be in subjection to your own husband; that, if any obey not the word, they also may without the word be won by the conversation of the wives;

While they behold your chaste conversation coupled with fear,

Whose adorning, let it not be that outward adorning of plaiting the hair, and of wearing of gold, or of putting on of apparel;

But let it be the hidden man of the heart, in that which is not corruptible, even the ornament of a meek and quiet spirit, which is in the sight of God of great price.

Likewise, ye husbands, dwell with them according to knowledge, giving honor unto the wife, as unto the weaker vessel, and as being heirs together of the grace of life; that your prayers be not hindered" (1 Peter 3:1-4, 7).

Mrs. Sugden: Now you answer this, dear, and let me demonstrate my meek and quiet spirit. And don't you dare forget verse 7.

Dr. Sugden: I observe your meek and quiet spirit. I will now proceed. This is one of the portions of the Word of God that needs little *explanation*, but it does need *to be promoted*. I think all of us know what a meek and quiet spirit would be.

It is interesting that the woman is to adorn herself. Did you know that this is the Greek word from which we get our word "cosmetic?" It is also the word from which we get the orderliness of the universe. It is the word that means that you live an orderly life, and that you dress orderly. Isn't that lovely? It takes in every aspect of a woman's life; what kind of person she is to be.

The husband is to dwell with her, and to give her honor. This means that once in a while he opens the car door for her when her arms are full of bundles. It means that he holds the chair for her when she sits down. It means that he gives her preference in his life. I think it is a plain and wonderful passage for husbands.

There are many great things in the Bible about the home and the family, but this is absolutely one of the greatest. It calls for the balance of the husband and the wife as they live together. And isn't this great? They are heirs together of the grace of life!

Mrs. Sugden: And if you husbands don't do that, your prayers will be hindered.

Dr. Sugden: Yes, they will. You will not have your prayers answered.

223. Hats

What has happened that women don't wear hats in church anymore? I am referring to 1 Corinthians 11:5-15.

Dr. Sugden: Hats got expensive.

Mrs. Sugden: You have to realize that there are cultural backgrounds for some of the biblical commandments. Women were supposed to worship with their heads covered, because if a woman went without a hat or without her head covered, it meant that she was almost a harlot. She was free for any man along the street. If her head was covered, it meant that she was in subjection to her husband.

It doesn't mean that now. It is different today. But if any woman wants to cover her head, I think it is all right. It is a choice that women have.

Dr. Sugden: I think that is true, dear. Many things we read in the Word of God are related specifically to the day in which the Word was written, but they covered all time and meaning. What it says is that here is a woman with her head covered, who lives in subjection to her husband. It is amazing that our society knows very little about this today. We have lost something of that which the covering of the head taught.

Mrs. Sugden: I would not defy any church. If I went in and their custom was to cover their heads, I would wear something on my head. When we were in El Salvador in Central America, the women all had their heads covered. So I always put a scarf over my head. I would not defy those people. It is not right to do that. If anyone feels that the head should be covered, they should do it. But I don't think we should be critical of others.

Dr. Sugden: In Israel I had to wear a scarf when I went into their places of worship. I was a sight!

224. Responsibilities of a Pastor's Wife

What are the responsibilities of a pastor's wife?

Dr. Sugden: I knew this question would come sooner or later.

Mrs. Sugden: And I didn't write this question, either. Actually, a pastor's wife has no responsibilities, because she is not hired by the church. However, underneath there are many responsibilities, because everyone has expectations for a pastor's wife.

But this question goes on, "What advice would you give to someone who is young and inexperienced at being a pastor's wife?"

Pastors are trained for their position, and pastor's wives have no training at all. I have jotted down a few things.

Dr. Sugden: (She has only two pages.)

Mrs. Sugden: The only way I can give any advice is from the mistakes I have made. You learn from your own mistakes, and you can learn from the mistakes of others.

First of all, pay attention to your own spiritual life. It is very important that you maintain a spiritual life of your own, because many pastors' wives (and I know this from talking to them) depend on their husband's spiritual life. You can't do that. You need to study the Word of God. You need to have your own prayer life. You need to have your own devotions—and that is the most important thing about your life.

Second, you need to be a good wife and keep a good home. You are the first lady of that church, wherever you are, and you need to maintain a good home. You are an example for the other women. You'll find that out after you get there. Whether you want to be or not, you just are. Therefore, it is very important for you to keep your home and your children. That is your next responsibility: your home, your children, and your husband. So, be a good wife.

Then, be involved in the work. I think it is very important for a pastor. Books are published that are written by pastors' wives that say, "Do your own thing. You don't have to be involved in the church." Well, it is all right to do your own thing if you are in the will of God, but *be sure* that *it is* in the will of God. That is very important.

You should use your spiritual gift. I know some pastors who won't let their wives do anything in the church because "she is my wife.'' But they expect other women in the church to do things. I think that a pastor's wife should exercise her spiritual gift, whatever it is.

Now, not all pastor's wives have the same gift. But, like the preachers tell everybody else, "If you don't use your spiritual gift, you will lose it." Pastors' wives should do the same. But don't try to do everything in the church.

Some churches expect the pastor's wife to do everything. Just use your spiritual gift. If it is music, use it, but not too much. If there are other people in the church who play the organ, let them play the organ, or the piano, or sing. Don't monopolize all of those things. That church has to go on after you leave.

Be a friend—but be a friend to all the people, not just a few. Some pastors and their wives have just close friends, and they are all they can see. Be careful about that. You are the pastor and the pastor's wife of the whole church, not just a few.

Show interest in your people and in their families. I have a prayer list. People give me their children's names. Perhaps their young people have gotten away from the Lord. Every Friday morning, everybody knows I pray for these young people who are away from the Lord. I have a long list. It is interesting how some can be crossed off because they have come back to the Lord. It is a thrilling experience. So be interested in them and in their families.

Then, have a hobby. I think it is very important for pastors' wives to have a hobby. It takes care of the stress. You are part of a very stressful life. I read an article once in a secular magazine about why so many pastor's wives have nervous breakdowns. One of the reasons they gave was stress. So you have to have a hobby to relieve stress.

Dr. Sugden: Do you want to know what her hobby is?

Mrs. Sugden: Swimming is one of my hobbies, and it is the best exercise in the world. When I swim I forget all the stresses of life.

Dr. Sugden: Stay on top, dear. Stay on top.

Mrs. Sugden: I'm not a great swimmer, but I do stay on top. And then I have the Detroit Tigers, you know. Everybody thinks that is the only thing I know are the Tigers, but I know a few things besides them. It takes off the stress, except right now when they're not doing too well.

Have good communication with your husband. But keep the

confidences of your people. Be careful about that. If you go gabbing about everybody to everybody, your husband is not going to communicate to you. He won't trust you. That is the reason you should not get too friendly with anyone in your church.

I have known pastors' wives who have been too friendly with some people and told them everything. You know what those people do? They tell everybody else. Just keep things to yourself.

These are a few things concerning the duties of a pastor's wife.

Dr. Sugden: Only a word to say that I have lived with Mrs. Sugden for over half a century, and she does exactly what she said.

Mrs. Sugden: Because I have made so many mistakes.

Dr. Sugden: Not really, dear. But it is important for a pastor and his wife to be together in their work. Pastors in pastors' conferences say to me, "Do you tell your wife about what is going on? We wouldn't tell our wives anything."

I said, "Well, my wife knows everything."

They said, "You tell her what is happening?"

Of course. How is she going to pray for me? How is she going to pray for the church? How is she going to help in the work?

You see, a husband and wife out there are a team. Their work together is what is going to help the church through the passing years. Mrs. Sugden has time to do things that I don't have time to do. She can talk with women. She can help these ladies, and she is noted for her candor. She simply tells them and it works that way. So it's good, dear. Thank you.

225. Woman's Place in the Church

This is controversial, but it is in reference to the woman's place in the worship service of the church. In our church women often open the service, lead in prayer, read the Scripture, lead the singing, and serve communion. I am not comfortable with all of this, and I wonder if I am wrong. Any Scripture verses would be helpful.

Mrs. Sugden: I will be unbiased, won't I? I think that the men should be in charge of the worship service. The man is the head of the home. Did you know that? He is the spiritual leader of the home. If I went into a church and saw women running the worship service, I would wonder what has happened to the spiritual life of the men. They are supposed to be spiritual leaders.

I know the Bible says, "But I suffer not a woman to teach, nor to usurp authority over the man" (1 Timothy 2:12). I teach a couples class. You have to compare Scripture with Scripture, because in Ephesians 5:22 it says, "Wives, submit yourselves unto your own husbands, as unto God."

You have to put these together. My husband says that I am to teach couples. So how can I keep that one and also keep the other? I would be usurping authority over the man if I did not subject to him. I am in a predicament. So I teach couples. Teaching a Bible class is different. They had no Sunday school or Bible classes then.

I think you have to put Scripture with Scripture in the teaching. Our women teach on the mission field, and I am sure they teach men. We have our missionaries speak sometimes in our church, but to run a worship service—I just do not think it is scriptural. All right, dear, you take it from here. They would have to usurp authority over the man if they ran the service, wouldn't they?

Dr. Sugden: You will discover a definite procedure in the New Testament as to the running of the local church. Whenever I have anything to say about women, I am very careful about it. I realize that women were significant in the life of the Lord Jesus. Did you know that they supported His evangelistic tours? They gave, and they made it possible.

Did you know that they were the last ones at the cross? Did you know they were the first ones at the tomb to see if He had risen? And they played a real part in the life of the early church.

The Word of God says that they are not to usurp authority over the man, so the men's positions in the church are as pastors and deacons. Someone commented, "Would you have any ladies who would be deacons?"

In our church we have deaconesses, but we do not have women deacons. It is not in the nature and order of the church to have women usurp authority over the man, and they usurp authority when they take the positions that are given to men in the Bible.

So, in our house of God we have women teachers. I see nothing wrong with women teaching the Word of God. Think of Ruth Paxson. Dr. Harry Ironside was Brethren, and I remember him saying, "If I ever get the chance to hear Ruth Paxson teach the Bible, I will be on hand to hear her."

She was not usurping authority over him. She was teaching the Word of God. In order to usurp authority, she has to have a position in the church that was given to a man. The man was given the position of pastor, and the position of deacon. Outside of that, women can be used and greatly used of God in the church. But I think that men were in charge in the order of procedure and Scripture in the worship hours, according to the Word of God.

You will remember also that women were not permitted ever to speak in tongues in the assembly. It says, "Let your women keep silence in the churches" (1 Cor. 14:34). That would do away with half or two-thirds of the modern tongues movement —if women had nothing to say.

So Scripture is very important. People sometimes say to me, "Well, Pastor, you are very lenient because you have a wife who is gifted in teaching. You want her to teach."

I find no place in the Word of God that says women cannot teach. It would be wrong if Mrs. Sugden were ever to ask if she could be a deacon or to hold an office in the church. That belongs to a man, because she would be usurping authority over the man.

Mrs. Sugden: Let me say one word about teaching. I had a professor one time who said, "Women are born teachers; men have to learn." I thought that was quite true.

226. Women Teaching Men

In this day there are many women who are well qualified with Bible knowledge, having gone to Bible schools and seminaries. In situations where there are no qualified men to teach Bible truth to other men, do you think God would overrule 1 Timothy 2:12?

Dr. Sugden: If there are no qualified men, I have no question in my mind that God would use a woman. Aren't you glad? Now you ask, "Do you have any principle, any precedent?" Yes, I do. Who was that lady judge in the Old Testament?

Mrs. Sugden: Deborah (See Judges 4 and 5).

Dr. Sugden: Deborah. Normally, there would not be a woman judge in Israel. But in this situation God allowed one. There is a principle that seems to say that if there are no qualified individuals, or if they are qualified and refuse to do the job, then God will get the job done with someone else.

I think He does this on the mission field. Do you know that for forty or fifty years about 75 percent of the missionaries on the field were women? Do you know why? Because men didn't go. I heard that when I was just saved. My pastor was a retired missionary. He bemoaned the fact that no man ever went to the mission field. He had given his life, and then he came home to die. When he came back that was one of his cries: "Why aren't there any men who will go?"

Today men are going, and I thank God for it. But there seems to be a principle that when God has no qualified man, or when a qualified man does not do it, then God will use a woman as He did Deborah.

BIBLIOGRAPHY OF
RECOMMENDED BOOKS

Question
Number

178 Biederwolf, Wm. E., *The Second Coming Bible Commentary*. Grand Rapids: Baker Book House, 1985.

51 Breese, Dave, *Know the Masks of Cults*. Wheaton: Victor Books, 1975.

51 Boreham, F. W., *A Bunch of Everlastings*. London: Epworth Press, 1920.

51 _____, *A Casket of Cameos*. London, Epworth Press, 1924.

51 _____, *A Handful of Stars*. London: Epworth Press, 1922.

51 _____, *A Temple of Topaz*. London: Epworth Press, 1928.

178 Broadus, John A., *An American Commentary on the New Testament: Matthew*. Valley Forge, PA: Judson Press.

57 Bullinger, E. W., *Number in Scripture* Grand Rapids: Kregel Publications, 1974.

51 Candlish, Robert S., *First Epistle of John*. Grand Rapids: Kregel Publications, 1979.

51 _____, *Studies in Genesis*. Grand Rapids: Kregel Publications, 1979.

51 Carroll, B. H., *The Interpretation of the English Bible*. Grand Rapids: Baker Book House.

155 Duty, Guy, *Divorce and Remarriage*. Minneapolis: Bethany Fellowship, 1967.

51 Ellicott, Charles J., *Ellicott's Bible Commentary*. Grand Rapids: Zondervan Publishing Co., 1971.

21 Frazer, Sir James, ed., *The Golden Bough*, 13 volumes. St. Martin.

110 *The Fundamentals*, 12 volumes.

51 Gaebelein, Arno C., *Acts of the Apostles*. Neptune, NJ: Loizeaux, 1965.

51 _____, *Annotated Bible*, 4 volumes. Neptune: Loizeaux, 1970.

51 _____, *Ezekiel*. Neptune: Loizeaux, 1972.

51 _____, *Gospel of John*. Neptune: Loizeaux, 1965.

51 _____, *Gospel of Matthew*. Neptune: Loizeaux, 1961.

51 _____, *The Prophet Daniel*. Grand Rapids: Kregel Publications, 1968.

51 _____, *Psalms*. Neptune: Loizeaux, 1965.

51 _____, *Revelation*. Neptune: Loizeaux, 1960.

68 Gardiner, George E., *The Corinthian Catastrophe*. Grand Rapids: Kregel Publications, 1974.

57 Grant, F. W., *The Numerical Structure of Scripture*. Neptune: Loizeaux.

161 Gray, James M., *A Primer of Prophecy*.

51 Gunther, Peter F., compiler, *A Frank Boreham Treasury*. Chicago: Moody Press, 1984.

**Question
Number**

1   Ironside, Harry A., *First Corinthians*. Neptune: Loizeaux, 1938.
54   Kessler, Jay & Beers, Ronald, *Parents and Teenagers*. Wheaton: Victor Books.
51   King, Guy H., *A Belief That Behaves*. Fort Washington, PA: Christian Literature Crusade, 1971.
82   Koch, Kurt E., *Between Christ and Satan*. Grand Rapids: Kregel Publications, 1972.
82   _____, *Christian Counseling and Occultism*. Grand Rapids: Kregel Publications, 1973.
82   _____, *Demonology, Past and Present*. Grand Rapids: Kregel Publications, 1973.
82   _____, *The Devil's Alphabet*. Grand Rapids: Kregel Publications, 1972.
82   _____, Occult ABC. Grand Rapids: Kregel Publications, 1981.
82   _____, Occult Bondage and Deliverance. Grand Rapids: Kregel Publications, 1972.
114 Lewis, C. S., *The Problem of Pain*. New York: Macmillan, 1943.
58   Lindsey, Hal, *1980: Countdown to Armegeddon*. New York: Bantam Books.
58   _____, *The Late Great Planet Earth*. Grand Rapids: Zondervan Publishing House, 1976.
51   Lockyer, Herbert, *All the Men of the Bible*. Grand Rapids: Zondervan Publishing House, 1958.
51   _____, *All the Prayers of the Bible*. Grand Rapids: Zondervan Publishing House, 1958.
51   _____, *All the Prophecies of the Bible*. Grand Rapids: Zondervan Publishing House, 1958.
51   _____, *All the Women of the Bible*. Grand Rapids: Zondervan Publishing House, 1958.
54   Money, Royce, *Building Stronger Families*. Wheaton: Victor Books, 1984.
51   Morgan, G. Campbell, *Westminster Pulpit*, 10 volumes. Old Tappan, NJ: Revell, 1954.
51   Moule, H. C. G., *Studies in Colossians and Philemon*. Grand Rapids: Kregel Publications, 1977.
1   _____, *Studies in Ephesians*. Grand Rapids: Kregel Publications, 1977.
51   _____, *Studies in Hebrews*. Grand Rapids: Kregel Publications, 1977.
51   _____, *Studies in Philippians*. Grand Rapids: Kregel Publications, 1977.
51   _____, *Studies in Romans*. Grand Rapids: Kregel Publications, 1977.
51   _____, *Studies in Second Timothy*. Grand Rapids: Kregel Publications, 1977.
54   Narramore, Bruce, *Parenting With Love and Limits*. Grand Rapids: Zondervan Publishing House, 1979.

Question
Number

122 Patterson, Alexander, *The Greater Life and Work of Jesus Christ.*

54 Petersen, J. Allan, *For Families Only.* Wheaton: Tyndale House Publishers, 1977.

52 Pfeiffer, Charles F. and Harrison, Everett, eds., *Wycliffe Bible Commentary.* Chicago: Moody Press, 1962.

51 Robertson, A. T., *A Grammar of the Greek New Testament.* Nashville: Broadman Press, 1947.

51 Ryle, J. C., *Expository Thoughts on the Gospels,* 4 volumes. Grand Rapids: Baker Book House, 1977.

54 Schaeffer, Edith, *What Is a Family?* Old Tappan: Revell, 1975.

61 Scofield, C. I., *New Scofield Reference Bible.* New York: Oxford University Press, 1967.

51 Parker, Joseph, *Prayers for Worship Services.* Grand Rapids: Baker Book House.

51 Maclaren, Alexander, *Exposition of Holy Scriptures,* 17 volumes. Grand Rapids: Baker Book House, 1975.

51 Sparks, John, *The Mindbenders.* Nashville: Thomas Nelson Publishers, 1977.

53 Spurgeon, Charles H., *Evening by Evening.* Grand Rapids: Baker Book House, 1975.

53 _____, *Morning by Morning.* Grand Rapids: Baker Book House, 1980.

51 Sugden, Howard F. and Wiersbe, Warren W., *Confident Pastoral Leadership.* Chicago: Moody Press, 1973.

51 _____, *When Pastors Wonder How.* Chicago: Moody Press, 1973.

41 Torrey, R. A., *The Treasury of Scripture Knowledge.* Old Tappan: Revell, 1973.

51 Vine, William E., *Expository Dictionary of New Testament Words.* Old Tappan: Revell, 1978.

215 Weymouth, Richard F., *New Testament in Modern Speech.* Grand Rapids: Kregel Publications, 1978.

37 Whitcomb, John C., *Origin of the Solar System.* Phillipsburg, NJ: Presbyterian and Reformed Publishing Co.

37 _____, *The Early Earth.* Grand Rapids: Baker Book House, 1972.

37 _____, *The World That Perished.* Grand Rapids: Baker Book House.

37 Whitcomb, John C. and Morris, H. M., *The Genesis Flood.* Grand Rapids: Baker Book House, 1960.

80 Wiersbe, Warren W., *Be Free* (Galatians). Wheaton: Victor Books.

51 Wilson, William, *New Wilson's Old Testament Word Studies.* Grand Rapids: Kregel Publications, 1987.

55 Young, Edward J., *Thy Word Is Truth.* Grand Rapids: Wm. B. Eerdmans Publishing Co., 1957.

SCRIPTURE TEXT INDEX

SUBJECT INDEX